Michael Lydon's

Rock F

Portraits from the Rock

Chuck B

No one fully grasped what was h ...., Berry seemed to have an idea. Of all the musicians, he was the one who best recognized these new American kids, and he loved and encouraged them. With an extraordinary leap of empathy, he knew and expressed their feelings, and they understood themselves through him. His songs were hymns to a generation; he was a black poet singing the praises of being free, black/white, and under twenty-one.

B.B. King

"I wish they had something could measure the pressure inside a person," King said. "Like at times when you're in a strong mood, if you've been hurt bad by a gal or your best friend. It's like that when I'm playing and I know exactly what I want to play and it's a goal I'm trying to reach, and the pressure is like a spell. But I know this, I've never made it. I've never played what I hear inside. I get close but not there. If I did, I'd play the melody so you'd know what it was saying even if you didn't know the words. You wouldn't know when Lucille stopped and my voice began."

Janis

"It was the most thrilling time in my life. I mean, I had never *seen* a hippie dance before, man, and then I was up there in the middle of one. I couldn't believe it, all that rhythm and power. I got stoned just feeling it, like it was the best dope in the world. It was so sensual, so vibrant, loud, *crazy!* I couldn't stay still; I had never danced when I sang, just the old sit-and-pluck blues thing, but there I was moving and jumping. I couldn't hear myself, so I sang louder and louder, by the end I was wild."

Grateful Dead

Jerry Garcia: "There's just no way to put that idea, 'save the world,' into music; you can only *be* that idea, or at least make manifest that idea as it appears to you, and hope maybe others follow. And that idea comes to you only moment by moment, so what we're going after is no farther away than the end of our noses. We're just trying to be right behind our noses."

(Continued on next page)

(Continued from previous page)

The Rolling Stones on Tour

In the crowd at Altamont: There are the dancing beaded girls, the Christlike young men, and smiling babies familiar from countless stories on the "Love Generation," but the weirdos too, whose perverse and penetrating intensity no camera ever captures. Speed freaks with hollow eyes and missing teeth, dead-faced acid heads burned out by countless flashes, old beatniks clutching gallons of red wine, Hare Krishna chanters with shaved heads and acned cheeks. A shirtless black man stands in the center of a cheering circle. "I have in my hand," he barks, "one little purple tab of 100 percent pure LSD. Who wants this cosmic jewel?" A dozen hands reach out eagerly. "Who really wants it?" "I do, I do, I want it, me, me, me." "Going, going, gone to that freaky chick with the blue bandana." He tosses it to her, and reaches again into his leather bag. "I have in my hand one cap of mescaline, guaranteed organic..."

portraits from
the rock 'n' roll pantheon

ROCK FOLK

BY MICHAEL LYDON

CITADEL UNDERGROUND

Citadel Press
Carol Publishing Group
New York

CITADEL UNDERGROUND

First Citadel Underground Edition, October 1990

Originally published by The Dial Press, New York, 1971.

A Citadel Press Book
Published by Carol Publishing Group

Editorial Offices   Sales & Distribution Offices
600 Madison Avenue   120 Enterprise Avenue
New York, NY 10022   Secaucus, NJ 07094

In Canada: Musson Book Company
A division of General Publishing Co. Limited
Don Mills, Ontario

Manufactured in the United States of America
ISBN 0-8065-1206-7

Some chapters of this book appeared in slightly different form, in the following magazines and newspapers: *Ramparts* ("Chuck Berry," "The Rolling Stones"); *The New York Times* ("Jimi Hendrix," "B. B. King," "Janis Joplin"); *Rolling Stone* ("Smokey Robinson," September 1968; "Carl Perkins," December 1968; "The Grateful Dead," August 1969). Grateful acknowledgment is made for their cooperation.

INTRODUCTION TO THE CITADEL UNDERGROUND EDITION

Michael was always a little bit ahead of me.

We were in the eighth grade when we met, the fifth class of the academically forbidding and institutionally competitive Roxbury Latin School. From the start, I think, we felt a common bond; we were both alienated in ways we couldn't name yet shared instinctively; along with a patchwork crew of other classmates we rejected the premise of the school that the intellectual life was the only life worth living, that intellectual achievement was somehow quantifiable, generally at someone else's expense. And we both knew that we wanted to be writers. We just weren't clear on how you got there.

We voraciously devoured books: Salinger, Hemingway, Fitzgerald, John O'Hara (what did it mean when it said that he "frenched" her?). In the ninth grade we had an English teacher named Omar Shakespear Pound, who demanded of us that we *write*. He assigned three or four compositions every week, some free-form, some on specific topics, which met with a decidedly mixed reaction from a class that had been taught to regard creativity, and each other, with deep suspicion. One assignment was to write a story on the well-known proverb: Only a fool learns from experience. Another was limited to observation of a day in downtown Boston.

I remember reading Michael's stories and reportage with envy. I felt that he had a natural talent, I *knew* he had a natural talent that I could never aspire to, merely seek to emulate through hard work. I still remember, or think I do, his description of a little boy on Tremont St. on a Saturday afternoon, checking nervously, and repeatedly, in his pockets for change for the subway ride home. The graceful fluidity of his style, his preciseness of observation, what seemed like an almost instinctive combination of insight and compassion (he didn't even have to work at it), a romantic sensibility that communicated itself, like Hemingway's, in hard, glistening, concrete images— I hated him! I mean, of course, I was proud and envious at the same time, he was so clearly in possession of the inside track.

I didn't see much of Michael after high school until a couple of years after we had both graduated from college. By then he was a full-fledged "professional." He had just left *Newsweek* and was still integrally involved with a fledgling *Rolling Stone*, at whose birth he had attended. It was 1968, and we were both just waiting for the future to happen. I was consigning my novels to an indifferent universe without faith or much in the way of encouragement (save for the occasional typed rejection slip); I was writing about music a little bit, too, for underground publications like *Crawdaddy!* and the *Boston Phoenix*, strictly as a hobby and as an outgrowth of my love for the blues. I don't think I could even have admitted to professional ambitions. Michael, meanwhile, was freelancing and actually making a living at it. Within a short period of time he had published in such previously unimaginable places as *The New York Times* and *Atlantic Monthly*; at a time when it would have been more logical to look in those pages for stories on whether the unexamined middle-class life was really worth living, Michael was writing wonderful idiomatic pieces about Carl Perkins and Chuck Berry and B.B. King, about the music that we had come, by different paths, to love so well. We exchanged passionately argued letters, as we had once exchanged childhood dreams and ambitions; we shared ideas, reminiscences, and philosophical beliefs, along with the occasional bruised feelings that can accompany any true baring of the soul. In one letter Michael wrote in typical evangelical fashion that he was looking forward to a day when Chuck Berry and Bo Diddley would be recognized for their conscious artistry, when "America [would] find out about them the same way they found out about Chaplin and Keaton." That was the core of Michael's mission, to call attention to the feeling that had been ignored in our formal education, and to the grace that underlay it.

Michael kept turning out remarkable work, full of that same sense of wonder and appreciation that I think has always characterized his writing, that presents its subject as something intrinsically rare and reassuringly commonplace at the same time. For a long time I thought I just wanted to publish my novels—and, in a way, I still do. But Michael's dedication not just to the writing life, but to The Life that gave rise to this particular version of the writing life, challenged my thinking, changed it to a degree, and eventually, I guess, won me over. His seeming self-assurance, on and off the page, his almost messianic sense that we—he, the music, a generation—were really *going* somewhere, was as much a matter of envy to me, and as far beyond me, too, in a way, as his composition on going shopping. When *Rock Folk* was published in 1970, in a format that scattered graceful, eloquent photographs amidst a graceful, eloquent text, it represented the first flowering of a generation of writers who had discovered new worlds. It served as a beacon brightly signaling: *It can be done*. I know that's how it was for me, because I was working on my own first book when it came out, and while its publication didn't cause me to abandon my efforts, it did cause me to redouble them.

I'm sure there are lots of things that can be faulted about our outlooks then and now. Sometimes I think back to when Michael and I were in high school and aspired to be wise guys together, to act out existential fantasies. Later, it seems to me, we each cultivated a sense of wonder, two self-styled "kids" in their twenties eagerly setting out to explore unknown cultures in a literary mode. But however naive or romantic our separate sensibilities may have been, I think they echoed an enthusiasm which school had not been able to drill out of us—which *no one* should allow education to drill out of them. I don't know that you could find a sharper, or more graceful, portrait of Carl Perkins anywhere than you will find in *Rock Folk*. And what a treat to meet B.B. King before he was —well, what a treat to meet B.B. King at any time, but what a privilege to be vouchsafed a glimpse of him before he was so universally, and iconographically, acknowledged. The shadowy presence of Chuck Berry, the arduous pleasures of the Rolling Stones on tour: Michael's portraits continue to ring true, because the writing is so true. For all of his exuberance there is always that intuitive grasp of the moment, the sharply etched detail, the portrait that threatens to burst out of its frame.

I talked to Michael the other day. We don't see each other that often, but it seems as if we will never run out of things to say and share. Michael is a full-time musician now and a part-time writer, but he, and I, are still pondering many of the same issues, to no more effect than idle delight. He has nearly completed a book about reading and writing called *Real Writing*, which includes vivid and illuminating essays on Balzac, Dreiser, George Eliot, and Henry James. It seems so funny to look back on a shared lifetime of crisscrossed experiences and ideas. Sometimes when I think of Michael, I think of his unabashed fervor for the cultural revolution of the '60s alternating with acute moments of self-doubt. Sometimes I remember my parents dropping him off at church when he stayed over on a Saturday night in high school, or staying over at his house and finding myself in the midst of this great, noisy world of lively talk, intellectual disputation and older siblings. One often wonders how one got to a certain point in life—and how anyone else might have got there, too. It's always struck me as odd that Michael and I (and Nashville producer Jim Rooney, too, just a few years ahead of us at the same tiny school) should all have ended up in the same unlikely corner of a multifarious cultural universe. But I suppose it's no more surprising than anything else, than any other realization, or thwarting, or diversion of childhood dreams. The important thing is to hang on to at least some aspect of the dream, as Michael proves over and over again in his book.

Peter Guralnick
March, 1990

Peter Guralnick is the author of *Feel Like Going Home*, *Lost Highway* and *Sweet Soul Music*, a trilogy on American roots music. He is currently at work on a biography of Elvis Presley.

CONTENTS

To my father, Patrick Joseph Lydon
and
To my brother, John Theodore Kevin Lydon

Beatrice!
Beatrice!
Paradiso is opening.
WE ARE AT THE GATES OF THE CHERUBIC!
—Michael McClure

ACKNOWLEDGMENTS

I now see why authors say it is impossible to thank by name all the people who helped them: It's the truth. This book was written over the past year and a half. I talked about it with dozens of editors, writers, musicians, friends, and just about everybody I met in that time, and they all contributed. Thank you.

My thanks, also, to the many people I interviewed, not only the main subjects of the chapters, but their friends and acquaintances too. I couldn't have done it without them; their courtesy and interest made it a pleasure.

For their help in encouraging me to write, I want to thank my brother Christopher whose confidence in me got me past hurdles I never could have crossed alone; Seymour Peck of *The New York Times,* a brilliant and hard-working editor whose patience, care, and kindness are unmatched in his trade; and Paul Williams, a pathfinding writer, true friend, and revolutionary.

Luckily for me, the actual production of the book was done by people close to me in heart and spirit: my agent Anita Gross; Lorraine Shapiro, herself a fine musician, who copy-edited it; Ellen Mandel, a co-conspirator at all times, who took the flap photo; and especially my editor Bob Cornfield, who read and re-read it all with a critical eye and understanding mind.

My gratitude, too, to my brother Frank Bardacke and my fellow communards of Fisherman in Berkeley where I spent much happy time, and, last and most of all, to Elk, California. My thanks to its people, young and old, who have been helpful neighbors and fine friends; to its calm spirit of free community; and to its hills and beaches, woods and fields. In barely beginning to tell me their secrets, they have already taught me more than I ever hoped to learn.

Michael Lydon   Elk, California   May, 1970

JIMI HENDRIX: 1945–1970

I could sit up here all night and say thank you, thank you, thank you, you know . . . I just want to grab you, man, and just umm kiss you, but, dig, I just can't do that . . . so what I want to do, I'm going to sacrifice something right here that I really love . . . don't think I'm silly doing this, 'cause I don't think I'm losing my mind—last night, ooo whew, but, wait, wait, today I think everything is all right, you know, so I'm not losing my mind. This is just for everybody here, this is the only way I can do it, okay? . . . Don't get mad, don't get mad, no.

> *—Jimi Hendrix, before he burned his guitar at the*
> *Monterey Pop Festival, June, 1967.*

"Rock Star Jimi Hendrix Dead at Twenty-four—that's what the papers said. Sad enough and true. Jimi Hendrix is dead, he was twenty-four, and he was a star, as brightly gorgeous a star as ever graced rock 'n' roll music.

And yet, and yet. Twenty-four is very young to die, even for a blues singer, and Jimi Hendrix was more than a star. He was a genius black musician, a guitarist, singer, and composer of brilliantly dramatic power. He spoke in gestures as big as he could imagine and create; his willingness for adventure knew no bounds. He was wild, passionate, and abrasive, yet all his work was imbued with his personal gentleness. He was an artist extravagantly generous with his beauty.

My words do not do him justice; his own do. "I want to hear and see everything." "Stone free, to do as I please." "Excuse me while I kiss the sky." It does not do to read them; they must be heard as he sang them, his voice urgent, earnest, and humorous over his quirky rhythms while his awesomely inventive guitar splashed sound in dazzling hues.

It will be years before we know enough to know how fine an artist he was.

Jimi Hendrix was a blues man, perhaps the greatest

of his generation. Like his predecessors in that noble line, Robert Johnson, Sonny Boy Williamson, Otis Redding, and all the rest, he was a man, proud and boldly sexual; a musician, a dedicated innovator who immeasurably widened the range of the electric guitar, and a dreamer, alternately dazzled and plagued by visions he could not help but pursue.

Some say the blues are declining. The evidence is that they are the most vital art form in the world today. Each decade has brought new syntheses, each generation new leaders. Jazz has never strayed far from its blues roots, and the blues mainstream, after successfully negotiating the move from Southern country to Northern city in the forties, took over electric music in the fifties.

Rock 'n' roll was, as everybody knew at the time, blues with a beat, created by men whose potency had wider scope than sex alone. "I'm a MAN," sang Bo Diddley, "spell it M, A, N," announcing the end of the days of black boyhood, while Chuck Berry in his zoot suit, eyes burning with liberated anger, dared to take on Beethoven. White kids, first country boys like Carl Perkins, then high school teen-agers like Bob Dylan, responded with their own blues. Then gospel singers began to sing the blues and that got called soul music. They even started "reelin' and rockin' " in England.

Jimi Hendrix was heir to all those traditions. The first music that turned him on was Muddy Waters; he heard the Hit Parade and the Top-40 in his Seattle high school. He was in the Air Force like Johnny Cash, and he toured with the first gospel rocker, Little Richard, and also with Ike Turner, who long before that had inspired Chuck Berry in St. Louis and even before that had signed B. B. King to his first contract in Memphis.

The black show biz world, however, had an automatic ceiling that Jimi could not accept. His friends, who are still playing the same anonymous honky tonks, advised caution, but Jimi split for New York to break into the big time. Greenwich Village, with its interracial underground of artists and heads, was more congenial than bleak Harlem, where competition was cruel for the smallest gigs. Challenged by the freedom of Bob Dylan's imagery, he began to write his own songs, though at first he didn't dare sing them. When, in 1966, he was invited to England, where experimental black musicians have been given gratifying welcome since Duke Ellington's first visit in 1933, he accepted at once.

In six months he and his Experience (bassist Noel Redding and drummer Mitch Mitchell) had conquered the English pop scene. Monterey in June, 1967, was his triumphant return home. A psychedelic hootchie-kootchie man, swathed in red and orange, he was magnificent, at the very edge of the believable and totally real.

His first American tour that summer (part of it on a bill below the Monkees), was not exactly a failure, but the second the following winter was a complete success. A year after the Monterey Pop Festival, Jimi was *the* superstar of rock, second only to the inactive Beatles, Rolling Stones, and Dylan. A dazzling stage performer, he also made masterful records: *Are You Experienced,* a no-holds-barred debut; *Axis: Bold As Love,* a mellow second; and *Electric Ladyland,* both bluesy and surreal.

Stardom is never an easy life, and rock stardom in the late 1960's was as tough as any created by stage or screen. A lot of people wanted pieces of Jimi for their scrapbooks. He was arrested and tried for possession of drugs in Toronto in 1969, but was acquitted. He, like Janis Joplin, who died two weeks later under similarly tragic circumstances, was at the center of an energy vortex as powerful as the music he created. (Janis, said Al Aronowitz, "was on the same wavelength as Jimi Hendrix.") The Experience faltered and broke up. Jimi experimented with several groups of musicians to get something new that worked. A few performances (one recorded), as the Band of Gypsies were the result; they were good but not good enough. Last spring The Experience came together again. At times it was brilliant, yet it too was often close to breaking up again. He and the group were resting from a European tour when he died. Friends say he had a troubled and unhappy summer.

The records are left, as well as, luckily, two superb films of him onstage—at Monterey and at Woodstock where, with a surgical and demonic precision, he gave "The Star-Spangled Banner" what it deserves.

I met him twice as a reporter; both times he was open and friendly. I would like to think his death accidental; if it was not, it is not hard to guess the strains he was under. I just wish Jimi Hendrix were alive and making music today.

INTRODUCTION

The first gig my friend Jim Payne ever played was twelve years ago, the day his first drum kit came in the mail. His group, the Deltrons, had an audition with an agent. They went down to his office, and Jim set up, trying to figure out what to do with all the goddamn knobs. He never got the heads tightened. "I was playing, and the drums were going flummpf flummpf, but I didn't know, man, and neither did the agent. We got the date."

Now Jim is living in a tiny Lower East Side basement apartment, practicing four hours a day with the rumble of the furnace in his ears, working on his paradiddles and ratamacues and listening to Elvin Jones and Tony Williams. For six months he's been with the Blues Magoos and is beginning to get some studio work. He's twenty-seven and a drummer, determined to make music all his life.

Between that first gig and now, he went to private school, Yale, business school, and even did a short stint in the Navy before he was declared unfit for service. "It's funny," he said one night we were sitting up smoking and listening to records. "In school I'd spend days digging James Brown and Bobby Bland, scared I was wasting time. They had me convinced studying time was *real* time, but now it seems like I was becoming a musician *all* the time."

On the way he's been in eleven bands he can remember (the Deltrons, the Invictas, the Dukanes, Little Achilles and the Heels, December's Children, the Five Card Stud, Prince Lala and the Midnight Creepers, the Kents, Jim Ground, Birdsong, and Congress), played clubs from the Canadian border to Daytona Beach, made a record that was number one for a few weeks in North Carolina, taken lessons from Philly Joe Jones, and never made a dime more than subsistence living. One group he was in failed an audition at the Peppermint Lounge; another played on a bill with Otis Redding in Central Park. One of his producers was Richard Perry, now a big shot at Warner Brothers. Perry, then a hustler in the Brill Building, showed the group a picture of Tiny Tim and said that someday he'd be a star; the group took one look at the photo of the freak (this was 1965), one look at Perry, and split.

In high school in Bridgeport, Connecticut, he played Italian clubs. "One night we played with a group called Tony Cee and the Centuries. Tony Cee—his name was Carangerola or something—was just out of jail, and when the cops came 'cause of the noise, he picked up his guitar and amp and ran out the backdoor shouting, 'They're not gonna get me, the motherfuckers,' his cord trailing behind him.' " In college the Dukanes had three black kids singing with them, and they did debutante parties. "The spades couldn't believe all the food and jewels, and they'd fill up their pockets from the dishes of Benson and Hedges that were always around. A year later black power got to them, and they wouldn't play with us anymore."

Hank Ballard was a star when Jim began drumming, and his groups did tunes like "Work with Me, Annie"; in Daytona ten years later Ballard was touring on his own, a has-been who didn't know it, and Jim's band backed him up. One summer he played Air Force stations in Greenland, fell in love with the girl singer (who later joined a nunnery), and met the leader of an all-girl band who played army bases regularly and did a pimping business on the side.

Rhythm and blues has always been his main bag. When the Beatles came out he thought they were amateurs, and he liked "psychedelic" music even less. Now he listens to anything, picking up ideas from whatever he hears. As a teenager he and his buddies were kicked out of a Jimmy Reed concert because they were white; in college he haunted the Apollo but was still outside the scene. One of his tightest buddies now is a black tenor sax player who used to lead James Brown's band.

One guy he played with is now a Thom McAnn shoe salesman, others are mechanics, lawyers, doctors, or insurance men. Very few are still musicians. "It's hard making enough bread, but even harder telling yourself it's worthwhile. Music starts out as fun, but who can believe it's gonna be what you're gonna *do*, dig? So many cats end up doing standards in crummy cocktail lounges or at weekend dances, but to avoid that, you really have to keep your shit together and be lucky."

Rock 'n' roll music is made by people like Jim Payne. There may be a select few who escaped the frustrations of disapproving parents, endless burns, dead audiences, cancelled gigs, flopping records, repossessed equipment, and broken groups, but all share the decision to make their lives making music, whatever the cost or gain. There are thousands of them, playing little clubs here and there, filling in at studios, working in music stores part-time, and taking whatever jobs come their way. They play in house bands if they can't stand the road, take to the road when there's nothing they can stand about home. Some savor memories of the time they played at this big theater or in that top band; others are still plotting for their moment; still more are just gigging because they dig it. Every record you ever heard was made by somebody, and if you liked it, probably the guys who made it were having a good time too.

Many have been friends. At home in Elk, in London, Berkeley, San Francisco, Los Angeles, New York, New Haven, Boston, Memphis, and even Pendleton, Oregon, I've run into them and spent hours talking, remembering, laughing, and listening to them play. They tend to be good cats, generous, unassuming, and cheery in a worldly sort of way.

Although this book is called Rock Folk, it concentrates not on those folk but on rock 'n' roll stars, artists of particular distinction and popular success. Given the star system that dominated rock from its inception to the end of the 1960's, and my special love for the musicians included, the form seemed appropriate. Through its individual portraits I hope the book gives a sense of what rock 'n' roll is and where it came from. Yet that "given" star system was also a distortion, the errors of which are thankfully becoming ever more apparent. Not only were the stars once unknowns and still are dependent on the skills of unknowns (including technicians of many kinds), they are obviously no more or less human than you and me; the worm that may eat of a king may eat of a teen idol too.

Some musicians may be snobs or fools, but most have long known that simple truth. In *Don't Look Back* Bob Dylan is seen at a peak of rock 'n' roll arrogance; yet in the opening

sequence, when he is petulantly flipping cards printed with key words of "Subterranean Homesick Blues," two cards have words not in the song. They read DIG YOURSELF and IT'S HARD. Stardom in rock is in fact a double distortion because the music's main import (message is not quite the word) has been the celebration of our humanity, sensual and spiritual, together. Rock 'n' roll artists make that especially precious kind of music designed to entertain, music whose form springs from the desire to please the people, to become, quickly and with joy, the song not only of the singer but of the listener as well.

The musicians and their music have succeeded to a remarkable extent. In fifteen years rock 'n' roll has become the music of millions, embraced by a worldwide generation as an extention and reflection of themselves. It has grown and changed as its makers and listeners have grown and changed, and is today, more than ever, a reliable truth teller, a self-generated standard of honesty and legitimate authority. Of its essence good-time music, it has been an inspiration and guide in the search for truly better times. "When you are listening to a rock 'n' roll song the way you listen to 'Jumping Jack Flash,'" said Peter Townshend of the Who, "that's the way you should really spend your whole life." I do believe we are getting a little closer all the time.

There is still much to be done. The star system still exists; some fans still worship, and there are stars whose superficial privileges conceal from themselves (if from few others) the fact that they too are part of the rock 'n' roll working class. The cupidity of the industry continues as well; not only does rock 'n' roll showbiz overcharge the listener and underpay most artists, it also taxes both listener and artist by perpetuating the fad and star systems for its own profit. All the record companies and promoters do for their money is make the music available; that service has been proven to be possible at low or almost no cost. Once that lesson is taken to heart and acted upon, the power of the industry will be severely weakened and rock 'n' roll further liberated.

After that (or right now, for that matter), the only remaining step will be for you and me to start singing our own songs. Everyone in this book from Jim Payne to Mick Jagger worked hard to make his own music. All of them, despite their trials, and even despite what wealth they made, gave and continue to give that music freely. It only seems right that if we like them, we should try our best to give it back. Our own song might not come out in music; then again, it might: no one in this book was anymore of a musician before he started playing than anyone else is. If you just can't see yourself making music, try dancing to it, or at very least get in there and dig it. They say it will get you higher and it will.

CHUCK BERRY

The white youth of today have begun to react to the fact that the "American Way of Life" is a fossil of history. What do they care if their old baldheaded and crew-cut elders don't dig their caveman mops? They couldn't care less about the old stiff-assed honkies who don't like their new dances. . . . All they know is that it feels good to swing to way-out body-rhythms instead of dragassing across the dance floor like zombies to the dead beat of mind-smothered Mickey Mouse music. . . . To the youth, the elders are Ugly Americans; to the elders, the youth have gone mad.

—Eldridge Cleaver, "The White Race and Its Heroes,"
Soul on Ice

Let's welcome to the Fillmore the man who made contemporary music, CHUCK BERRY." Deafening applause. Berry leapt out into the spotlight and up to the mike.

"All right?" he shouted.

"All right!" said the crowd.

"All right?"

"All right!"

"All *right!*" said Chuck. "Yeah! It's nice to be back in California; I needed the sunshine." Rippled laughter. He took a pose, chopped a quick chord, and sang.

> *Up in the morning and out to school*
> *The teacher is teaching the golden rule . . .**

He had on a black shirt, loose yellow slacks, and yellow shoes with chains across the instep. His long hair was tousled, his face already stippled with sweat.

> *Working your fingers right down to the bone,*
> *And the guy behind you won't leave you alone . . .*

*From "SCHOOL DAYS" by Chuck Berry. © 1957 Arc Music Corp. Used with permission of the publisher.

1

His mouth was tight, his eyes looked out from a frosted distance behind his high Indian-proud cheekbones.

> *Back in the classroom, open your books,*
> *Gee, but the teacher don't know how mean she*
> *looks . . .*

Streetcorner hustler and show business dude, he was arrogantly elegant and vice versa, and his staccato choruses rolled out in whiplash strands.

> *Soon as three o'clock rolls around,*
> *You finally lay your burden down,*
> *Close your books, get out of your seat,*
> *Down the halls and into the street . . .*

The crowd—the standard long-haired, dropped-out, stoned-out mob—made little squeals as the song moved toward the climax. The red Gibson flashed in his hands like a rapier, his body lithe as a willow.

> *Drop the coin right into the slot,*
> *You've gotta hear something that's really hot,*
> *With the one you love you're making romance,*
> *All day long you've wanted to dance . . .*

As the crowd breathed a near audible yeah of recognition, Chuck chanted what had been, a decade before, the prophetic incantation of a generation.

> *Hail, hail, Rock 'n' Roll!*
> *Deliver me from the days of old,*
> *Long live Rock 'n' Roll!*
> *The beat of the drum so loud and bold,*
> *Rock, Rock, Rock 'n' Roll!*
> *The feeling is there body and soul.*
> —"School Days"

He commanded the stage, magically looking not a day older nor one whit changed, creating a live rerun of a time gone by. To comprehend that handsome figure was to re-experience an era, to retaste adolescence and the fifties; and the memories he evoked were memories of himself. The presence of Chuck Berry made past and present one, packed into one complete moment the

2

feelings of a young lifetime growing up in America, and then opened up the way to exaltation, to digging who you had been, who you were, and who you could become . . .

> *Hail, hail, Rock 'n' Roll!*
> *Deliver me from the days of old.*

To get to Berry Park, Chuck Berry's combination amusement park/country club near Wentzville, Missouri, you take Interstate 70 about forty miles out of St. Louis and get off on Highway 61. It's the same exit as for Hannibal, and it's real Huck Finn country, corn and bovine lushness shadowed by massive clouds and pervaded by a damply buzzing August heat. Off from 61, Highway Z angles through Wentzville, past the Kroger and Ben Franklin stores, across the railroad tracks and by the grain elevator ("THE FARMERS OF THIS STATE BUILT AND PAID FOR A LOT OF ELEVATORS BUT THIS ONE THEY OWN," a fading sign proclaims). Then it cuts out into the country and takes you the last five miles to the park.

Chuck has lived in a house hidden on the Berry Park grounds for about six years—since he got out of jail. The house is well appointed for his hobbies—with a guitar-shaped swimming pool, a darkroom, a videotape machine, a professional recording studio—and he lives there in self-sufficient semiseclusion. On one hand still a public person, he is the park's full-time host and manager as well as barbecue chef for the big catered parties held there. He tours actively, playing between fifty and one hundred dates a year, and in the past three years he has recorded five albums.

On the other hand he is a virtual recluse. Until he returned to Chess Records in late 1969 after a three-year absence, he delivered his albums to Mercury Records as finished tapes for them to press and distribute; otherwise, he avoided the company. "Don't want to complain," complained a Mercury executive, "but yeah, he's a stubborn guy, living in the boondocks, taking no advice. Set in his ways, I'd call it. Sometimes he won't even return phone calls."

Berry has cut his touring down to quick trips to the job and back to Wentzville by himself, taking only a guitar and a small suitcase. "I'm proud to say that if you call me in the morning, and if there's a plane going to where you're at, I'll play and please you in the evening," he said not long ago. In San Francisco he stays at the Civic Center Hotel, a decaying fleabag whose only virtue is that it is directly across the street from the Fillmore West's stage door. Room clerks say he seldom leaves his room during the day, and after the last show he streaks to the airport to catch an overnight plane back to St. Louis.

If Berry has close friends, none of his acquaintances know any of them, and no one has seen him in his old St. Louis haunts for a long time. He has given only two interviews in years, and in those, while being polite, he kept to bare facts and ornate rhetoric, taking no stands and telling only what he wanted told. His publicity biographies skim over his life, dwelling on details like his love of homemade chili, strawberry shortcake, and "relaxing at a good movie." Unlike some stars who play an intricate striptease for their public, Chuck Berry is dead serious about his privacy and, consequently, is successful in defending it.

His guard does come down a little in Wentzville. Everybody in town (pop. 2,700) knows him by sight; he's been coming to Wentzville all his life to visit cousins, and he's often seen wheeling through in one of his powder-blue Cadillacs. It's been Caddies for a long time, but once he had a '58 Ford, black with chromed dual pipes, skirts, a Continental spare kit on the back, railroad air horns on the hood, and one of those tops that dropped back into the trunk. "Straight nigger machine," says a Wentzvillian.

The townspeople find it hard to figure Chuck. They're not proud of him, and there's never been anything like a Chuck Berry Day. They're curious, but with him that's a frustrating occupation. Not that he's unfriendly, people say, no sir. He had the senior class out to his park for their spring picnic last year for free, just like he let the school use his movie theater in town for the school play, and he even did the lights for it himself. He's always come by the proms and Legion Hall dances when he could to do some of his old tunes, and now that he owns the Corner Bar, he plays there a little most Friday nights. And he even lets "Dialogue Wentzville," the interrace meetings of the Human Development Corporation, get together at his place.

It's just that you never get to *know* him. He doesn't put his name to anything; most folks don't know half the things he's doing. Secretive, some call it, saying that "this ex-con rock-singing nigger's gonna buy up the whole place on the sly, and then where'll

4

we be?" A few parents were worried about letting the school kids go out to the park ("he was in jail for a sex crime, you know"), but the kids had a great time, especially when he let them use his videotape machine. He's never done anybody in town any harm—in fact, just the opposite. He's friendly when you meet him, never aloof; it's just that, well, you never know what he's thinking. "What's he come way out *here* for, when he could be living it up in St. Louis, Chicago, anywhere?"

Berry Park is no Coney Island, and there are no tacky signs for it on Highway Z, just one gothic-lettered placard. It is almost a country club—wide lawns and cool glades; a swimming pool, barbecue pit, tennis courts and boating ponds for the afternoon, a dance hall for the evening, and a small lodge if couples want to spend the night. A few years ago it was *the* place for St. Louis blacks, but now Chuck's name is less of a draw. The park is still popular, though, and with a good crowd it could be the "swing city" Chuck likes to call it.

The Sunday afternoon I got there the dull grey sky had discouraged picnickers, and it was deserted. I paid my three dollars to get in and had a hamburger sitting alone by the pool, which the lifeguard was methodically cleaning. A few waitresses were giggling by the grill. Otherwise, silence. Chuck's secretary came out and said Chuck knew I was coming, then disappeared without saying she'd find him. It was nervous work sitting there, as it was my third and necessarily final try for an interview. The first time, at the Fillmore, he had said to come back the next night, "but I won't tell you anything you don't know." The next night, after a half-dozen monosyllabic replies, he had snapped, "I don't rap about myself," and walked away. The stillness at the park seemed a bad omen.

Chuck didn't appear, and a waitress named Carol offered to show me around. From the fishpond we saw Chuck cutting weeds by the lodge, and walked toward him. He walked away; we followed and were catching up when he turned. "Carol, go back to work," he said evenly. "You, follow me." He led me to the parking lot. "Now," he said—his brown eyes were nut-hard spots in a polite black mask—"I'm gonna be real busy today, no time to talk to you at all. So you'll please leave." Pause. "Anyway, the park is reserved today for a private affair and no other guests are allowed. Do you doubt my word?" I said I didn't, but I did.

5

He went to the grill and got me my three dollars. I stood holding it, baffled and angry. He waited a fraction of a second, showing a smile that went no further than his mouth. "Standing in the sun ain't my shot, so . . ." And, acting rather than speaking, he turned back to his work.

"I got my public life and my private life and they is different," he had said at the Fillmore, but the frozen rage behind that mask at Berry Park was more than the annoyance at a reporter's intrusion. "Yeah, he can be moody sometimes," said a motel desk clerk. "Maybe he's an eccentric artist?" Maybe so.

"Hail, hail, Rock 'n' Roll/Deliver me from the days of old." When he wrote that fourteen years ago, did he think of rock as a delivering angel? Berry's intent is unfathomable, but the lines mean what they say. Whether he had foreseen it or not, that angel had done its job for kids like me.

But what had it done for him?

> *His mother told him, "Son, someday you'll be*
> *a man,*
> *An' you will be the leader of a big old band,*
> *Many people coming from miles around,*
> *Hear you play your music when the sun go down,*
> *Maybe someday your name will be in lights,*
> *Saying 'Johnny B. Goode' tonight"*
> *Go, go, go, Johnny, go*
> *Johnny B. Goode**

—"Johnny B. Goode"

In the spring of 1955, Charles Edward Anderson "Chuck" Berry was a blues singer-guitarist in St. Louis, Missouri. Twenty-eight years old, dashingly handsome, and a flamboyant showman, he had gotten a trio together (with Johnny Johnson on piano and Ebby Harding on drums) and did steady weekend work at the Cosmopolitan Club (later a grocery, now a club again, called the Cosmo Hall) in East St. Louis. Having finished the night course at the Poro School of Beauty Culture, he was also a hairdresser and "cosmetologist," and he wasn't sure which one was the moonlight job. No one expected the blues to support a man, and Chuck had a wife and two daughters, so it was nice to have a trade to fall back on. Anyway, both occupations were a big

---

*From "JOHNNY B. GOODE" by Chuck Berry. © 1958 Arc Music Corp. Used with permission of the publisher.

Chuck Berry at the peak of his career, about 1957

step up from the assembly line work he had been doing before at the G.M. Fisher car body plant.

He wasn't a star ("Nobody pays you no attention 'round here till you gets your first Cadillac," says a bluesman still active in East St. Loo), but the music had new possibilities. Ike Turner had just come up from Mississippi and was the talk of the town. Before Ike, blues in St. Louis had been almost an amateur business, done for a few bucks a night on a pick-up basis, and no one thought much about repertory or instrumentation. But Turner had a *band* that played *arrangements,* as near as could be note-for-note copies of hit records. Still small time, but now the small time was aping the big time. Chuck took it a few steps further.

"Chuck was always thinking progressive," recalls Gabriel Hearns, a trumpeter-disc jockey who now runs a dirty movie house in East St. Louis. "His music had a zing to it nobody else had. And professional—he made his guys wear uniforms and be real neat. Not even Ike was doing that. Chuck was a perfectionist, always had the best equipment, even bringing his own mikes to a job. Things had to be right, and, man, that was always Chuck's way." A city kid exposed all his life to normal American culture, Berry could also play a wider range of music than the country-born bluesmen, moving easily from country blues to the ballads of Nat "King" Cole and Louis Jordan (his idols), or even to a country and western tune. "You gotta remember," says Gabriel, "radio wasn't like it is now, each station only playing one sort of thing. They had hour shows of everything, so if you could play blues and ballads and country and novelty numbers, you reached more people. Chuck was versatile that way."

Ambitious too—"There was hungry cats and satisfied cats," said another musician, "and Chuck was among the hungriest"—but that wasn't new. One of a carpenter's six children, he grew up in Elleardsville (the 'Ville, natives call it), a quiet, black St. Louis neighborhood of small brick houses and tree-lined streets. His family were sober middle class, devout choir members at the toney Antioch Baptist Church, but Chuck was a feisty, eager boy. Quick-witted and quick-tongued, he was always in trouble and as quickly out. "Smart as a whip, Chuck," say's a lady who grew up with him. "Everybody knew he'd amount to something, leastways that's what *he* always said, but you just didn't know what."

8

Like every other black kid with more brains than patience, Chuck didn't know either. He had taken up guitar in high school, but not seriously. What could he do? Trying out the role of the young criminal, he got caught in a clumsy robbery attempt and was sent to reform school for three years. When he came out in 1947, twenty-one years old, he still didn't know. In 1955, after over seven years of waiting and working, hoping and wondering, he thought maybe the break had come. He had written a few songs he liked and could get up the fare to Chicago, so like hundreds of hopefuls before and since, he went up to the South Side, blues capital of the world.

From there on it reads like the storybooks. The greenhorn in the big city, Berry went to hear the big star Muddy Waters, who, with typical generosity, let him sit in for a set. Impressed, Waters told him to go see "Leonard." That was the late Leonard Chess, the founder of Chess Records which had and still does have the Chicago blues scene in its pocket. Berry went to Chess with a tape he had made on a borrowed recorder in St. Louis: "Wee Wee Hours," a mellow blues he had written, and "Maybellene," a novelty number based on a country tune he had rewritten and given a boogie-woogie beat. "We thought Maybellene was a joke y'know," recalls Chuck's old pianist, Johnny Johnson. "Took the name off the hair cream bottle. People always liked it when we did it at the Cosmopolitan, but it was 'Wee Wee Hours' that we was proud of, that was *our* music."

Leonard Chess, who died suddenly in October, 1969, knew better. A tough businessman who had started out selling records from his car, he knew his break had come too. Having established a solid base of bluesmen whose work sold only to blacks and paid only his basic costs, he was developing black talent that could make it in the far richer white market. He wasn't alone. King, Federal, Specialty, Savoy—all small independents that had signed the young black artists the big companies wouldn't touch—were working on making the race breakthrough. They knew that they were sitting on a gold mine, that if white kids could just hear the music, they'd go crazy. Closer to the grass roots than the major record companies, they had already seen the beginnings.

"When I used to go on the road with the black acts I was handling in the forties, they didn't let whites into the clubs,"

9

says Ralph Bass, an A&R man who worked for several independents before going to Chess about ten years ago. "Then they got 'white spectator tickets' for the worst corner of the joint, no chairs and no dancing, and the tickets cost more too. But they had to keep enlarging it anyway, 'cause they just couldn't keep the white kids out, and by the early fifties they'd have white nights sometimes, or they'd put a rope across the middle of the floor. The blacks on one side, whites on the other digging how the blacks were dancing, and copying them. Then, hell, the rope would come down, and they'd all be dancing together."

In the forties the music never left the ghettoes; by the fifties it was occasionally being cleaned up and recorded by white artists. The originals seldom got on the air because the radio stations, often tied in with the major companies like Columbia, RCA, and Decca, refused to play the "off-brand" records, as the independent labels were then patronizingly called. By 1955, however, there were a few DJ's who wanted something more adventurous than Mitch Miller. Alan Freed was the best known; he had just invented the name "rock 'n' roll" to replace "race music," had moved his show from Cleveland to WINS radio in New York, and was getting unbelievable ratings playing this "rock" to white teenagers.

"I told Chuck to do 'Maybellene' for us and give it a bigger beat," said Chess a few weeks before he died. His office was decorated with gold records, four by Chuck Berry. "I liked it, thought it was something new. I was going to New York anyway, and I took a dub to Alan and said, 'Play this.' The dub didn't have Chuck's name on it or nothing. By the time I got back to Chicago, Freed had called a dozen times, saying it was his biggest record ever. History, the rest, y'know? Sure, 'Wee Wee Hours,' that was on the back side of the release, was a good tune too, but the kids wanted the big beat, cars, and young love. It was a trend and we jumped on it."

If you were thirteen years old or thereabouts in 1954, World War II was a uniform in a closet and dirty stories of Jap tortures; the Korean War was games of "get the gook" on the neighborhood Heartbreak Ridge; and national prosperity was your own bedroom in a new suburban house and an allowance from Dad, who always said *he* had never gotten one. Blacks were "colored people"; you probably thought that "nigger" wasn't polite anymore. The Supreme Court decision on school integration was a headline. You and just about everybody else were normal—had crew cuts, chinos, sport shirts, and loafers. There might have been a few hoods around with D.A.'s and garry belts, maybe even switches and juvie records; you envied them, but they were scary, maybe even illegal, and, anyway, pretty dumb. Cars, like the two-tones and hard tops and hydramatics, were keen, but you had to be sixteen to drive. Same to smoke. Too old for Little League and the kiddie stuff on television, radio, the movies, or in general, you were too young for everything aimed at adults.

Music was no exception: Perry Como, Eddie Fisher, Teresa Brewer, Patti Page; "That's Amore," "Doggie in the Window," "Stranger in Paradise," all coming from the radio ballroom shows—it was *okay,* and you hummed the tunes when they were on Your Hit Parade. But they weren't done for *you,* and they didn't do anything *to* you. They were just there, coextensive with and as natural as that Ike-WASP-peace-and-prosperity consensus which was threatened only by a few commies at the top, no swelling from below. There was nothing to criticize because there was little else to know. Then you heard "Shake, Rattle, and Roll" and you knew there were worlds "they" hadn't told you about.

"Shake, Rattle, and Roll," then "Rock Around the Clock"—fast, hard, so much energy in a curve of power that started low and swept up and up to an *explosion!* Daddy-o? Daddy-*cool!* "They" didn't like this music and its dirty dancing at all, but the door had been opened and the children were getting beyond their control.

1955. In somebody's basement you heard "Work with Me, Annie" and "Annie Had a Baby"; you sniggered, and marveled that "they" allowed it (or that this Hank Ballard had such daring). After that Georgia Gibbs's cute "Dance with me, Henry" was not only a laugh, but a top-off that "they" had known about this new world and hidden it from you. Then came "Maybellene" and this skinny, jumpy, colored cat called Chuck Berry. Craaazy! A beat that made Bill Haley pallid, nutty words like 'motivatin',' and a story about a guy chasing a Cadillac in his beat-up Ford to catch his girl. Oh, the triumph of the "V-8 Fo'd" leaving the "coupe de ville" sitting like a "ton of lead." But even more, it was the drive of the thing, the two minutes of *rush,* pure manic intensity, that sucked you in.

11

1956. "Blueberry Hill," "Fever," "See You Later Alligator"; Little Richard, who could sing higher and lower and faster than anybody; Carl Perkins, who laid it right out: "Don't step on my blue suede shoes." The Platters, Mickey and Sylvia, Frankie Lymon, Gene Vincent, and then Elvis, the King, who was in flesh, spirit, and aura more perfect, more beautiful, more *you* than you could ever, ever hope to be. He sold about seven million records that year, and it was all over. "Lisbon Antigua" was a big hit that year too, and maybe you bought a copy, but it didn't matter, 'cause rock 'n' roll was here to stay, the good times had begun to roll, and you sang with Chuck Berry, "They're really rockin' in Boston, Pittsburgh, P.A., Deep in the heart of Texas, and 'round the Frisco Bay."

Chuck was rockin' too. The record he cut in May was number one in July, and in August he was signed to a tour that circled from New York to Florida and back, "one hundred and one nights in one hundred and one days," remembers Johnny Johnson. "Whew, the feeling it was to go from nothing to top bill in a few weeks I could *never* explain." There was only one way to rock success in those days. Get a hit, go on the road and push it; as it fades, put out another and go out and push that. No time to lose because the sun was finally shining so you'd better start raking that hay, man; who knows when it's gonna cloud over again. Chuck Berry worked like that for five years, touring with every star in the big package shows, appearing in three rock movies, and playing on all the TV "bandstands."

On stage he was magic, a glittering, rubber-faced jester who sang you the truth and made you laugh. Every star danced as he sang, but only Chuck had the "duck walk" that he first did at the Brooklyn Paramount in 1956. His back stiff and straight, he'd squat down over one heel, his other leg sticking out in front, and with his head at a weird tilt, he'd bounce across the stage, holding his guitar before him like a machine gun. All the way across, playing like mad, then back to the mike and coming in shouting right on the beat. The whole theater would gasp, then rock with applause. He had done the impossible with perfect grace.

"We didn't see too much of Chuck in those days," says Johnson. With Ebby Harding, Johnny's now back where he started, playing pick-up piano around St. Louis on weekends and

working in a steel foundry during the week, but he recalls his days close to stardom without regret. "Yeah, we'd work at night, then Chuck would be in his room until the bus left writing new tunes. Always writing; never seen such a hard worker."

After "Maybellene" came "Roll Over, Beethoven," then "School Days," and then one begins to lose track: "Sweet Little Sixteen," "Rock 'n' Roll Music," "Johnny B. Goode," "Oh Baby Doll," "Memphis," "Reelin' and Rockin'." Tune after perfect tune, Berry's revved up voice and slashing chorded guitar, Johnson's rippling, darting piano (the best piano in all of rock 'n' roll), Harding's sledgehammer drumming, and above all the lyrics—words of comic daring, cynicism and naïveté, sexuality and mock innocence, bizarre invention and banality. All of it, right down to the technical production that made the records sound as if they were recorded in a garbage can, all of it great rock 'n' roll music...

> Let me hear some of that rock 'n' roll music,
> Any old way you choose it,
> It's got a back beat you can't lose it,
> Any old way you use it,
> It's gotta be rock 'n' roll music,
> If you wanna dance with me.*
>
> —"Rock 'n' Roll Music"

Heady days, that first lindying era of rock. In retrospect it is astonishing how fast it happened. Early rock is replete with instant success stories like Chuck Berry's: complete unknowns making smash hits their first time in a studio. Which means that the music filled a gargantuan need that neither artist nor audience knew existed. Rock's excitement in 1954–55–56 was that of love at first sight. Some date rock back to Fats Domino's first million seller ("The Fat Man") in 1948, or even to "Open the Door, Richard" in 1946; the music does go back that far, but it really became rock 'n' roll when it met its response. Neither music nor phenomenon alone, rock 'n' roll is a mass sensibility.

That sensibility not only came from nowhere and spread everywhere, but was so natural to those who shared it that it was impossible to explain. Nonbelievers made comic hay of the tongue-tied rock star and the girls who could only shriek "Eeeiiie I *love*

*From "ROCK 'N' ROLL MUSIC" by Chuck Berry. © 1957 Arc Music Corp. Used with permission of the publisher.

him!" when asked why they loved Elvis. But how else to say it? Fifteen years ago you couldn't say why you loved rock 'n' roll, not only because you didn't know why (and you didn't), but also because maybe you didn't dare. And maybe "they" couldn't understand your love for the same reason. For that sensibility was not just sensuality, speed, and rebellion, but also *black*—how much still isn't clear, but more black than anyone was willing to admit in 1955. The rock 'n' roll sensibility meant that on some level white kids who were trying to find their own identity were identifying passionately with black music, doing it barely consciously but therefore without any self-conscious distance. And not just identifying passively, but creating a new identity between white and black.

The medium of the process was the music, which from the first was a racial and musical hybrid. "Blues plus country equals rock" is a cliché inadequate to express rock's heritage or its sharing. Rock was willing to use almost every kind of American music known. Little Richard emerged as a star for white teenagers straight from a black gospel showbiz that until then few whites knew existed. The Platters, on the other hand, were a very funky version of the Mills Brothers and the Inkspots, who had long been popular with whites. Elvis was tremendously influenced by blues singers (he had been one of those kids in the white spectator section), but he added a white punk sexuality all his own. His "Hound Dog" had first been done by Big Mama Willie Mae Thornton, but it had in turn been written for her by two young, white songwriters from New York, Jerry Leiber and Mike Stoller, who, in turn again, had just reworked an old blues. Carl Perkins's "Blue Suede Shoes" was the first record ever to top the rhythm and blues (black) and popular (white) charts at the same time. All the stars, white and black, toured together, and heard and were influenced by each other's music.

In short, a black-white music and white kids who said, "Yeah, that's how *I* feel." That was rock 'n' roll. You often didn't know if it was white or black; it just had to have a beat so you could dance to it. Not that 1ace had disappeared, not at all, but white kids had started to go to the same shows as blacks, to listen to the same music, and to love it for the same reasons—because it was funny and sexy and strong and lifted you up to a place where you *knew* that being a square from dullsville was a lot less than what you could be if you kept on rockin'. However inarticulate, it was a perception new enough that nervous adults said it was lewd, possibly a Communist plot, and caused riots; or, alternatively, they took pains to dismiss it as a silly fad. And they did indeed have something to fear; rock 'n' roll was the beginning, however tentative, of a state of mind (if not way of life) beyond race in America. If only while they danced, those outrageous rock 'n' rollers, in pink and black peg pants, toreadors and pin curls, were integrated Americans.

No one fully grasped what was happening, but Chuck Berry seemed to have an idea. Of all the musicians, he was the one who best recognized these new American kids, and he loved and encouraged them. With an extraordinary leap of empathy, he knew and expressed their feelings, and they understood themselves through him. His songs were hymns to a generation; he was a black poet singing the praises of being free, black/white, and under twenty-one.

He got it all, the whole cast of characters, their every plight and possibility. There was "Sweet Little Sixteen" . . .

> *She's got the grown up blues,*
> *Tight dresses and lipstick,*
> *She's sportin' high-heel shoes,*
> *Oh, but tomorrow morning,*
> *She'll have to change her trend,*
> *Be sweet sixteen,*
> *And back in class again.**

And her parents . . .

> *Oh, Mummy, Mummy,*
> *Please may I go,*
> *It's such a sight to see,*
> *Somebody steal the show,*
> *Oh, Daddy, Daddy,*
> *I beg of you,*
> *Whisper to Mummy,*
> *It's all right with you.*

—"Sweet Little Sixteen"

*From "SWEET LITTLE SIXTEEN" by Chuck Berry. © 1958 Arc Music Corp. Used with permission of the publisher.

Chuck Boyd

And the typical teen . . .

Yeah, I'm doing all right in school,
They ain't said I've broke no rule,
I ain't never been in dutch,
I don't browse around too much,
Don't bother me, leave me alone,
Anyway—I'm almost grown.*

—"Almost Grown"

*From "ALMOST GROWN" by Chuck Berry. © 1959 Arc Music Corp. Used with permission of the publisher.

And high school romance . . .

> *I remember so well,*
> *Back when the weather was cool,*
> *We used to have so much fun,*
> *When we were walking to school,*
> *If we stopped off to hear*
> *The latest songs they sing,*
> *We'd just make it in*
> *Before the bells would ring.*[†]

—"Oh Baby Doll"

He knew the drag of stupid jobs . . .

> *Working in the filling station,*
> *Too many tasks—*
> *Wipe the windows,*
> *Check the tires,*
> *Check the oil,*
> *"Dollar gas!"*
> *Ahhh,*
> *Too much monkey business*
> *For me to be involved in it.*[‡]

—"Too Much Monkey Business"

And cars, cars that could fly, cars to cruise in, neck in, speed in, listen to rock in, and cars of pure fantasy, like the one he demanded in "No Money Down" . . .

> *Well, Mister, I want a yellow convertible,*
> *Fo' Do' de ville*
> *With a continental spare*
> *And wire chrome wheels;*
> *I want power steering,*
> *And power brakes,*
> *I want a powerful motor,*
> *With jet off-take;*
> *I want air condition,*
> *I want automatic heat,*

[†]From "OH BABY DOLL" by Chuck Berry © 1957 Arc Music Corp. Used with permission of the publisher.

[‡]From "TOO MUCH MONKEY BUSINESS" by Chuck Berry. © 1956 Arc Music Corp. Used with permission of the publisher.

I want a full-length bed
In my back seat;
I want short-wave radio,
I want TV and a phone,
You know I gotta talk to my baby
*When I'm riding along.**

Powering it all was a terrible urgency to detail the world of the kids he sang to, down to those "wallets filled with pictures," so everyone would know it was real and beautiful, and no joke. "Roll over, Beethoven, an' dig these rhythm and blues!" Comically arrogant, yes, but also Chuck Berry's gauntlet thrown down in challenge to conventional culture and all its sacred cows; it was the ultimatum to the Ike-WASP consensus from the barbarian at the gates, the first warning that "they" had better dig this energy that was making their children dance.

Berry poured out the energy tour after tour, record after record, and the strain told. He always had to work hard at rock, said Leonard Chess, keying himself up to get the rhythm right, to get the power going. One part of him still preferred the blues, the easier, more comfortable groove, and he even asked Chess if he could record blues under an alias. Chess said no ("Rock was what was happening"), but on most of his albums there are one or two instrumentals that show a soft and pensive Chuck Berry. Rock, he always felt, was "commercial." "On tour," Johnson says, "we did the hits, one after another, but sometimes if it was real late Chuck would relax for once, and we'd do some blues, runnin' on and on. But mostly Chuck was all business."

He never had a manager or the normal retinue of leeches politely called "aides," and the corporations that handled his money had no members outside his family. "There weren't many people Chuck trusted," said Chess. "He kept a close watch on himself. Never drank, no drugs. Took only his own advice. A showman, yeah, but inside a timid guy, fighting all the time." His St. Louis nightclub, Chuck Berry's Club Bandstand, was the fulfillment of a dream, but he ran it more as businessman than as genial host. A fulfillment too was the brick mansion he bought for his wife and children on the cul-de-sac where the cream of St.

*From "NO MONEY DOWN" by Chuck Berry. © 1956 Arc Music Corp. Used with permission of the publisher.

19

Louis black society live in enormous dignity. But he could be there only infrequently. He had many separate worlds, and keeping them separate required full-time control and no mistakes.

He made one. Late in 1959 a prostitute he had picked up while on tour in Juarez, and then brought back to St. Louis to be a hat check girl in his club, turned herself in to the police after he dropped her. She was, she admitted then, only fourteen years old, and Berry was arrested and charged with violating the Mann Act. Given a few sordid realities, the charge becomes absurd. The girl, a Spanish-speaking Apache Indian from New Mexico, had been a prostitute for a year and he hardly had "compelled, induced, and incited" her "to give herself up to debauchery," in the language of the indictment. And a man of Chuck's status doesn't have to bring his pick-ups home; it's probably true, as he insisted, that his real intent, which the law requires proven, was to learn Spanish because he thought songs in foreign languages were the coming trend (though he might have had a few other things on his mind as well). But the law and the public were not ready to take so worldly a view.

The case dragged on through two years and two humiliating trials, both in St. Louis. The first judge was so blatantly prejudiced, calling Berry "this Negro" or "whatever his name is," that his judgment was vacated, but the verdicts of both trials were the same: guilty. The implicit substance of the charge was expressed by the newspaper headline: "Rock 'n' Roll Singer Lured Me To St. Louis, Says 14 Year Old." "They" had always known that this dirty music was corrupting their children, and now they had caught a gaudy nigger with his pants down to prove it. "Is this the kind of man our children idolize?" Maybe if they could put him away in jail, they could believe that the answer to their own question wasn't yes.

Chuck entered the Federal Penitentiary at Terre Haute in February of 1962. It looked as if they had not only gotten him, but rock 'n' roll as well. It was the absolute end of an era which had passed its peak four years before. Buddy Holly was dead, and so was Richie Valens and the Big Bopper, all victims of the same plane crash. Elvis had come out of the Army a changed man, every trace of the young rocker smoothed away. Jerry Lee Lewis had been driven from the spotlight by a similar trumped up "sex scandal." Gene Vincent, Fats Domino, Little Richard—all were fading memories, replaced by anemic nonentities like Joey Dee, Bobby Vinton, and Chubby Checker. Chuck had hung on longer than any of the others, but even his clean, straight style had been corrupted by strings and choral back-ups in desperate attempts to keep up. The first rock 'n' rollers were now voting adults, and the jet-setters were twisting at the Peppermint Lounge. What had been fresh in 1955 had become formula, and then simply repetition. The crackle of that early da-DAH da-DAH rock beat became the endless drone of "pa pa oom mau mau, pa pa oom mau mau." Adventurous young musicians were playing folk.

And then, just as before, with the same out-of-nowhere bursting, it all happened again. Detroit, Liverpool, London, Los Angeles, San Francisco, and then everywhere, reelin' and rockin' on a scale that the fifties could not have conceived. The new stars were different; they were regular middle-class city kids who could have become lawyers or doctors or grown-ups of one accepted variety or another. But they didn't, and with a blitheness that was shocking, they said they didn't want to; they, and the kids who followed them, wanted to rock their lives away.

Without exception they acknowledged their debt to Chuck Berry. It was not just that they played his songs, but with their every act, they said that they had laid their burden down, closed their books, and made that trip out of the classroom and into the street.

"Never saw a man so changed," Carl Perkins said of Chuck not long ago. "I did a tour of England with him after he got out of prison. He had been an easygoing guy before, the kinda guy who'd jam in the dressing rooms, sit and swap licks and jokes. In England he was cold, real distant and bitter. It wasn't just jail, it was those years of one nighters, grinding it out like that can kill a man, but I figure it was mostly jail."

Everything had changed for Chuck when he came out. His club was gone, and so was his marriage, his fans, and his moment. There was nothing else to do but go back to work and figure out a new game, this time playing it with *no* mistakes. Leaving his wife and children with the house in St. Louis, he moved out to Wentzville and started Berry Park. He did a packed return concert in Detroit to start touring again, and made the charts a few more times with some of his greatest songs, including the rollicking "Promised Land." But those were probably (though Chess is not telling) tunes he had recorded years before that had never been released. His new songs were tired, often just updated lyrics sung over the music from his hits of nearly ten years before. Despite the fact that the Beatles, Beach Boys, and Rolling Stones were making hits with their versions of his songs, Chuck's own attempt at a comeback was a failure. DJ's played his early records as golden oldies but ignored his new ones, and without radio exposure Chuck as a contemporary performer disappeared from rock 'n' roll.

His response was to bury himself ever more deeply in Wentzville and get his business affairs neatly rationalized and entirely in his own hands. It would be impossible to estimate Berry's considerable wealth, but he has never been broke. His early records still sell, and the royalties from the countless "cover" versions by other artists, several of them million sellers in their own right, amount to a substantial income. To get more capital for the park, which quickly became his main occupation, Chuck left Chess Records and signed with Mercury for a $150,000 advance. He continued to take gigs when they were offered and his policy on payment was and is unswerving: $2000 a night, half to be paid in advance, the rest immediately before going on stage. A short-sighted policy perhaps (he refused to play at the Monterey Pop Festival, forgoing invaluable exposure, because he was asked to play free), but one that guarantees him a predictable income without forcing him to trust anyone.

"It's a ritual every time Chuck plays here," says Paul Baratta of the Fillmore West. "Chuck breezes into the office about five minutes before showtime the first night and says, 'Let's do our thing.' I give him a check, he endorses it. I count out the money, give it to him, then *he* counts it out, pockets it, and gives me back the check as a receipt. He says 'Mellow,' then goes on stage and knocks 'em out. We've done it so often now, maybe he'll wink at me, but it's still a ritual."

Berry's concert dates are becoming more frequent. After Bill Graham first booked him at the old Fillmore in 1967, Chuck started to get the "psychedelic" ballroom jobs. The new rock generation flocks to hear him play his old songs, but the more relaxed format allows him to do the long blues jams as well. As good a showman as ever, he makes every set a triumph. At forty-three, his duck walk is still a superbly graceful feat, and he always goes off stage to a standing ovation. He has no intention of stopping. "I asked him when he would retire," says Baratta, "and he said, 'When I get tired of playing or people get tired of hearing me play, and I think the latter will happen first. I have it figured. See, I'll never play, never *ever* play for less than $1000 a night. So some day I'll get a call from some twenty-two-year-old punk promoter and he'll say he really wants me but he can only offer $950. And I'll tell him, 'Congratulations, son, you've just become the man who retired the great Chuck Berry.' "

But that day is still years away. Berry, his contract with Mercury expired, has gone back to Chess. His first Chess album, *Home Again,* is brilliant. Maybe Chuck Berry will be back topping the hit parade. Who knows, and will it matter? What does revival mean in a world where music, preserved on plastic, never ages or is lost?

"This rock bit," Chuck said in a rare interview with Ralph Gleason, "it's called rock now, it used to be called boogie-woogie, it used to be called blues, used to be called rhythm and blues, and it even went through a stage of what is known as funk. . . . Names of it can vary, but music that is inspiring to the head *and* heart, to dance by and cause you to pat your foot, it's there. Call it rock, call it jazz, call it what you may. If it makes you move, or moves you, or grooves you, it'll be here. The blues rolls on, rock steady knocks, and they *all* are here now and I think they all *will* be here from now on."

Rock on, Chuck Berry!

David Gahr

CARL PERKINS

Seems like I could hardly wait till the day
*   that I got grown,*
I wanted to pull out of those cotton fields,
*   wanted to get out on my own,*
There's a whole lot about this big world I didn't
*   know,*
Seems like every place I turn I still got a row
*   to hoe.*
I got tired pickin' that cotton,
I got tired balin' that hay,
I got tired diggin' those taters,
I got tired workin' that way.*
                 —"I Got Tired"

"If it weren't for the rocks in its bed, the stream would have no song," said Carl Perkins with a comic dolefulness. He had just put down his well-thumbed copy of *The Power of Positive Thinking* and was staring out at the brown miles of Texas prairie that slipped unchanging past the Dodge mobile-home bus.

Carl, thirty-seven, his extensive baldspot covered by a rakish toupee and his front teeth rebuilt with a plate, was on tour with The Johnny Cash Spectacular. He's been working with Cash for four years now, sometimes playing lead guitar with John, and always opening the show with twenty minutes of uptempo pickin' and singin' to warm up the country crowds. He doesn't exactly have the "how the mighty are fallen" blues—his own days at the top were too brief, and steady work with the biggest country and western tour in the business isn't the bottom—but Carl has had his share of vicissitudes, and they've made him philosophical.

*"I GOT TIRED" by Carl Perkins. © Cedarwood Publishing Company, Inc., 1970.

"I'll tell you true," he said that sleepy afternoon as the bus rolled from Lubbock to El Paso. "I've been at the top of the bill and now I'm at the bottom, and there's no comparing 'em. The top'll beat the bottom every time. At the top you know the people came for you. At the bottom you're just somebody between the crowd and what they came for, and you gotta work real hard out there to make it seem worth it to yourself."

He got up to check why the new plastic top for his dune buggy was rattling where he had stowed it beside the stove in the bus's kitchen. He was nervous about it not only because it was, in all its pink metallic gleam, his pride and joy, but because Johnny had at first made him keep it outside lashed above the spare tire. Now Carl was sure Johnny would make him take it out again. He stopped the rattle with some wedged newspaper and slouched back into his seat.

"Oh, Carl, don't be blue," said honey-blonde and honey-voiced June Carter Cash. "Why, you know the people all enjoy hearing you. You're an indispensable part of this show—isn't he, John?"

"Sure is," said Johnny Cash, folding his sex-adventure paperback over his gut and edging his voice with mock sarcasm. "I don't know what we'd do without you, Rock King."

"Laugh," said Carl, "but that's what they called me, and that's what some still call me, the King of Rock 'n' Roll."

They all—John and June, guitarist Bob Wooten, bass player Marshall Grant at the wheel, and drummer W. S. "Fluke" Holland beside him—laughed and hollered. Carl went ostentatiously back to his book. He is a natural born straight man; his humble pride is his comic device. He reads *The Power of Positive Thinking* seriously, but it's like Mr. Peepers reading Charles Atlas. Yet he is never pathetic. "We all love Carl," June said that evening. "He's been through some hard times, but they've never soured him. Think what it means for a man who was number one to be working behind an old friend. Carl can do it because he's a big man."

Months afterward, late one October night in the grimy and soundproofed splendor of Columbia's East Fifty-fourth Street studios, Carl was recording with NRBQ, a young rock band with one record to their credit. He was there because a top Columbia executive, looking for something appealing to the "rock revival" market, suggested that NRBQ invite Carl to share the credits of their next LP. A brilliant stroke—Columbia teamed up two contracted artists whose sales had been unexciting to say the least; NRBQ got a chance to work with the real thing, and the ever-obliging Carl, still determined to make a comeback, was willing to ride the coattails of "New Rock" if that might get his music out again.

Carl Perkins, author of "Blue Suede Shoes," is today, if not an unknown, an unheard. As Jerry Lee Lewis likes to point out, rock 'n' roll's teenage fans (compared to blues and country audiences) are cruelly fickle: stop pleasing them and they forget you. Success in the popular charts was always a chancy thing for those white country boys who, working in a direction opposite that of Chuck Berry, reached the same synthesis of uptempo country and blues that was rock 'n' roll. Elvis was the only one of them who got himself a secure place outside of Nashville; the rest—Carl, Jerry Lee, Roy Orbison, Gene Vincent, Conway Twitty, Bill Haley (and probably Buddy Holly had he lived past his peak) got their meat and potatoes from the country market and their occasional Cadillac when they were lucky with the kids.

Record store clerks ask, "Who?" when you request a Carl Perkins album. DJ's with great golden oldie collections draw regretful blanks looking for his singles (many on 78's only), and some knowledgeable fans are sure he's dead. Some remember "Blue Suede Shoes" only as a big hit for Elvis. That it was—the opening track of his first LP, but the Pelvis's cover version is only one of the tributes to Carl's genius imbedded in rock 'n' roll history. Bob Dylan has said that his very first record, done for an obscure label in Minnesota, was Carl's "Matchbox." "Blue Suede Shoes" became a must song for every struggling rock band in the world; John Lennon, playing live for the first time with the Plastic Ono Band, announced that they would only play songs they knew because they hadn't rehearsed anything; then he and Eric Clapton swung immediately into "One for the money, Two for the show, Three to get ready, now, go, cat, go!" George Harrison, who later sat at the feet of Ravi Shankar, first idolized Carl's guitar. In fact, the Beatles recorded more Carl Perkins songs than any other writers whose work they covered in their early days—"Matchbox," "Everybody's Trying to Be My Baby," and "Honey Don't."

The Grateful Dead's version of "Sitting on Top of the World" is taken, says Jerry Garcia, a long-time Perkins fan, from Carl's recording of the country classic.

And the NRBQ, whose commercial gimmick is their "good old rock 'n' roll" image, had just released a single of "Sure to Fall," one of Carl's ballads, and now they were working on "Bopping the Blues" with the composer himself. NRBQ was in sloppy denim, but Carl had on a shiny grey mohair suit with Western Cut button pockets and a bright blue shirt. His cigarette, impaled on the twisted end of one of his guitar strings, bounced in place. Carl started running through the song softly, trying to remember the words. "All my friends are boppin' the blues, must be goin' 'round," he sang in a warm baritone, breaking it with tiny falsetto jumps. He picked out a few bars in the second chorus in his high and gently singing guitar style, and Steve "Fergie" Ferguson, NRBQ's lead guitarist, fell in behind playing rhythm, but as they began the third chorus, suddenly Fergie was playing lead, his quick and aggressive tone cutting through Carl, and Carl, just nodding his head, fell back into the rhythm slot. The rest of the band started playing too, a little too loud and hard, but making a pretty fair facsimile of the original Sun sound. The wound it up with a flourish, Fergie taking the final break. Carl slapped his guitar and grinned.

"Man," he said to Fergie. "You make me ashamed to take the banjo out of the case."

Fergie, a hairy redhead whose mouth is fixed in a perpetual sneer, protested mightily but in vain; Carl refused to give in. NRBQ's manager and producer Frankie Scinlaro called from the control room that it sounded great and they should do an immediate take. Carl asked for a mike to sing into.

"Oh, no," said Frankie over the intercom. "We'll do the vocal later."

"But I always play and sing at the same time; never recorded any other way," Carl said. "I get more feeling that way."

"Yeah, but we get a better sound if we can put the voice on as a separate track," replied Frankie.

Piano player Terry Adams added something about mixing and balance and told Carl it would be all right. Carl nodded again, and said it was okay by him if it was okay by them. After a few tries they got a good instrumental track, but as they finished it, bassist Jody St. Nicholas said he thought he had made a mistake.

"Oh, it won't sell if it's got a mistake in it," Carl said. "That's what old Sam Phillips used to say. But you should hear some of those early records Johnny used to make with Marshall and Luther—Man! One little bass mistake ain't nothing compared to them."

The band laughed and gathered around Carl to hear tell of Memphis and Sun in the early days. The rest of the night was like that, moments of work broken by Carl's drawled stories. At the end of a hot take of "Sorry, Charlie," he called to Frankie, "Man, if folks don't jump for that, they're dead. Sick won't take it. *Dead!* I'd hate to play that in a hospital. If a guy was in traction and he didn't have a heavy ass piece of lead on his foot, he'd be jumping." Carl told of Phillips's still secret tape of Elvis singing gospel tunes with Cash and himself, which, for sentimental reasons, he had held back when he sold all his Elvis material to RCA Victor, but since has never been able to release. And that rolled into a story of how Jerry Lee Lewis got his wild style.

"Jerry, when he started, he was people-shy. Johnny and I were on tour with him in Canada, his 'Crazy Arms' was just out, and he'd sit at the piano with just one corner of his face showing and play Hank Williams tunes. He came off one night in Calgary moaning, 'This business ain't for me; people don't like me,' and John and I told him, 'Turn around so they can see you; make a fuss.' So the next night he carried on, stood up, kicked the stool back, and a new Jerry Lee Lewis was born. And we regretted it because he damn near stole the show. Four nights later he was top of the bill."

And how he wrote "Blue Suede Shoes": "The easiest song I ever wrote, got up at 3:00 A.M. to write it when me and my wife Valda were living in a project. Had had the idea in my head, seeing kids by the bandstand so proud of their new city shoes—you gotta be real poor to care about new shoes like I did—and that morning I went downstairs and wrote out the words on a potato sack—we didn't have reason to have writing paper around. I didn't dare play because my two babies were asleep, and once you got those rascals asleep, you didn't wake 'em. When I told Sam about the song, first thing he said was, 'Is it anything like 'O Dem Golden Slippers'?"

The recording went on, not so smoothly as the talk. Carl suggested some tunes and arrangements, but was gentleman quick to drop his ideas at any show of opposition. NRBQ was running the session after all; Carl was the guest star, which meant he was flattered but never made to feel quite at home. If he was ready to play and NRBQ wasn't, he waited, but he jumped to be ready for them. Fergie kept taking most of the solos, and Carl did his manful best singing in the isolation booth, hiding worried grimaces as the earphones threatened to dislodge his toupee. The kids liked Carl and loved his music, but they weren't ready to go all out for it or him; no matter what they had learned from him, they had top billing.

"Maybe you could hold back a bit before the break," Terry called to Carl, "Then I can get some piano in, a thing I worked up with Jody."

"Okay by me," said Carl.

Midnight, then 1:00 A.M. It was hard work and they were rushing. "Great," said Frankie as they finished each track. "Keep it up." Carl wanted to get to bed so he could get back to Jackson the next morning—his wife's sister was in critical condition after an operation. They managed to get some nice music down—"All Mama's Children," one of Carl's tributes to rock 'n' roll, in particular—but there was no magic. Carl was polite to the end, but then he seemed the only one disappointed too. "You gotta keep at it," he said. "Can't wait for the hits to come to you."

Winding up about 2:00 A.M., he told his last story. The janitors were already pushing the mike stands into the corners, and Carl was packing his guitar and signing an autograph for the engineer. "Yes, sir," he said. "I met the Beatles. In England in sixty-four I heard I was one of their favorites. They invited me to a party and George asked me what I was doing the next day. I said, 'Nothing,' even though I was planning on going home, and the next morning a Rolls picked me up at my dingy hotel and took me to the studio. Ringo called me Mr. Perkins. 'That's my daddy's name, son,' I told him. He asked if I minded if he sang 'Honey Don't' and 'Matchbox,' and I said, 'Why, no, not at all, but just make sure those royalty checks get to Carl Perkins, Jackson, Tennessee, U.S.A.' They cut the tunes while I was there. I played on a cut they never released, but I liked the boys, and the checks got through, helped me through some tough times."

"Maybe that was the start of your comeback," said Terry.

"Yes, sir," said Carl. "Now you boys get out and sell some of this stuff, and maybe we'll all end up in the gravy."

"Blue Suede Shoes" was the fourth song Carl Perkins recorded, his first hit, and his greatest song. It's still his closing number, and though a hunting accident which shattered his left foot has cut his once hot-footed dancing down to little hops, he still brings it to rollicking life. "You can burn my house," he sings, standing in a fifties drugstore hood pose,

> Steal my car,
> Drink my liquor from an old fruit jar,
> Do anything you want to do,
> But uh-huh honey, lay off a them shoes,
> Don't you,
> Step on my blue suede shoes,
> You can do anything,
> But lay off a them blue suede shoes!*

It was a song that showed the way. With a great dancing beat, clean and snappy guitar, and funny-serious lyrics, it set rock's "teen feel" pattern of defiant and narcissistic self-assertion. Songs like "Blue Suede Shoes" literally created the Fifties Teenager; the hoods in their leather jackets and muscle T-shirts, who had dice hanging from the mirrors of their chopped, blocked, and dropped '51 Fords, who spent hours to get that Sal Mineo curl in their DA's, and slouched away Saturday afternoons at the picture show catching Marlon in "The Wild One"—they all loved "Blue Suede Shoes." Some radio stations played it for whole afternoons, and the millions of kids who heard it were suddenly linked and could say, "This song is us, and what we wanna say is: Lay off our blue suede shoes, daddy-o."

Carl achieved that by singing and playing his own song, the blues of a poor white kid from Tennessee growing up from the grinding poverty of the thirties and war years into the hope of the fifties. More flamboyant than conventional country stars, Carl and his comrades, punk kids then just like their fans, didn't have a chance to get into the big company studios in Nashville, so they went down to Memphis and Sam Phillips's Sun Records, which until they arrived had been almost exclusively a blues label. That was a minor revolution by itself: a new generation of white country singers finding a "nigger" label their natural home. Then they revolutionized Sun until the Nashville companies (in fact regional offices of New York-based firms), woke up and started buying them away from Phillips, who never quite adjusted to the big-time.

Carl never made it either—except for the few months before Elvis became an international phenomenon. The other country boys had a little more polish and a lot more luck, and Carl has lived his professional life in their shadow. The afternoon before the session, Carl sat in a New York motel room and told his story, his warm, soulful voice going on for hours as he sipped coffee and cracked his knuckles.

As far back as memory takes me, music is there. Before I went to school, I started fooling around on a guitar. My daddy made me one with a cigar box, a broomstick, and two strands of baling wire, and I'd sit and beat on that thing. My first real one a colored man gave me when I was five. See, I was raised on a plantation in the flatlands of Lake County, Tennessee, and we were the only white people on it. I played with colored kids, played football with old socks stuffed with sand. Working in the cotton fields in the sun, music was the only escape. The colored people would sing, and I'd join in, just a little kid, and that was colored rhythm and blues, got named rock 'n' roll, got named that in 1956, but the same music was there years before, and it was my music.

First day I went to school, I refused to go unless I could take my guitar. The teacher said, "We came to learn, not play, but now you brought it, so play." I got up on the first day and played "Home on the Range." I played in every class skit after that. Why, I was on the radio when I was in the fourth grade. Miss Lee, my teacher, took me the seventy miles to Jackson to WTJS. I sang two songs, "Home on the Range" and "Billy Boy."

32

We lived in Tiptonville and my daddy was a share-cropper. The night I was born my mom lay on a bed with no doctor but a granny lady named Mary. My daddy had double pneumonia on the next bed and almost died. He was always in bad health after that, later had a lung removed. They wouldn't give him good land on account of his health, but he did all he could. I had two brothers, Jay two years older, and Clayton two younger.

The shacks we lived in there are still up, three rooms— kitchen, living room, bedroom. We three brothers slept in the living room. It leaked, and I used to listen to the tones when it rained into the waterbuckets, singing, all different.

I was the poorest white boy in my school. There's a story from that time that still bothers me. (Y'know, some things happen you never forget and then you realize why people have bad dreams and hatreds deep inside. So you can't let 'em happen to your own kids.) I was in the fourth grade. One day there was a big pasteboard box by Miss Lee's desk. Kids were putting clothes in it. At close of school she called me to stay behind. I was afraid I had done something wrong. (See, I tried to be a good boy. I would have stole, but mom's faith brought us through trouble. In my mom I figure I have something some boys don't never get.)

Miss Lee said, "I don't want to make you feel bad, but it's a hard winter and your clothes are thin and the other boys gave you this." I looked through the box and saw these corduroy pants. I had never had any. I was wearing them a week later playing football with a kid. He came at me and it was my job to tackle him. I threw him pretty hard. He said, "You tackle me like that again, and I'll take back those britches." That stuck with me, and I said to myself, "With health and the good Lord's help, I'll never be like that again, to have to be good to somebody so he won't take his britches back."

Went barefoot in the summer, we had to. No electricity. We had a radio and every fall we'd get a battery—we bought everything in the fall. I'd listen to the Grand Ole Opry; Saturday's we'd stay up to nine o'clock and listen. I remember how sad I'd get when the battery started to fade; it would last about three months, so then I'd stay over with friends to hear the radio. White music, I liked Bill Monroe, his fast stuff; for colored, I liked John Lee Hooker, Muddy Waters, their electric stuff. Even back then I liked to do Hooker songs Bill Monroe style, blues with a

33

country beat. Colored man's rhythm—it's unbeatable; I can't do it. It's a soul type thing. They can make music on bucket lids; if a man broke a string, he'd just tie it back. High class instruments didn't mean a thing to them.

When I was fourteen we all moved to Jackson to get better land, because us boys were grown, and we got taken off welfare, got a good farm to sharecrop. I quit school after eighth grade, 'cause I knew if I didn't go to school, we could make a good living. Jay and I worked, and Clayton helped. In Jackson things were better. Four rooms, good roof, and we realized something from the crop.

That year I got my very first really good guitar. I went to a store and said I had no money but had a good cotton crop and would pay in the fall. That fellow's told me since he saw the honesty in my face and couldn't let me down. I got a $150 Les Paul, the one I cut my first record with. A friend of mine had an amplifier and he'd lend that to me. When I paid Mr. Towater, that was his name, for the guitar, I got me a Gibson amp and then paid for that the next year.

The man who taught me guitar was an old colored man, I can see him now, sitting on his porch. He taught me in Lake County. I'd ask him in the field, "Uncle John, you gonna play tonight?" "Maybe, if my back ain't too tired," he'd say. My Daddy'd let me go over for an hour. Uncle John'd get his old guitar out, and fill a pot with oily rags, then light it to make a smoke-screen to keep the mosquitoes away. John Westbrook was his name, the champion cotton picker on the plantation. He taught me how to pick cotton too. I could pick three hundred pounds a day, and, man, that's grabbin'. He said start at the bottom of the plant and move up, said it was all in the rhythm, keeping all your movements smooth, and starting from the bottom, you could see all the bolls as you moved up.

Other than John nobody taught me. If there was a song I liked, I'd try to catch some of the feel of it. I had a good memory for songs and was good at figuring how to get something off the radio onto the neck of my guitar.

And last year, you know what happened? I got a reception in Jackson, came in on a plane, and there were two thousand people standing in the rain. I thought maybe the governor was on the plane, but I saw my family and knew it was for me. They had

Carl Perkins Week, five days playing all my songs on the radio, and at a banquet at Lambeth College, they played my life from beginning to end, had people from my whole life. They had dug up on old pair of blue suede shoes and bronzed 'em on a plaque. The theme was "Blue Suede Turned To Gold." It was a night I'll never forget. They asked for a speech, and I had nothing planned, but I said this: "My mother taught me as a boy that love among people is the strongest asset the world has ever known. Tonight I've learned what true love really is. Jackson, Tennessee, chose me of all its people to bestow this great honor upon. If only I can live up to be the man you think me to be, I shall not die in vain." Then I started crying and couldn't say any more.

But I never would have made it without Valda. Valda's the baby of her family, and she is a fine, understanding woman. A lot of men say this about their women, but if every man had a woman like I have, we'd have a lot better men. Back when I was working at the Colonial Bakery, she said I'd make it, when we had nothing on the table. She'd always say I was the best in the whole world. Even when alcohol took hold of me and I stayed drunk for ten years, she stayed with me. She gave me four beautiful children; she doesn't even drive a car; she stays home. Not the woman for everybody, but when I come home, I stay home. I could never say enough about Valda. Anyone who knows me, knows my woman. They'll all tell you, "Carl's got one of the greatest little women ever lived." Roger Miller, Roy Orbison, Johnny Cash—they all stop, and she never gets excited. "You all will stay for supper, won't you," she says, and she knows how to cook. She cooks biscuits for breakfast; there's no toast in my house. The boys love to sop up the gravy with them. She's a good country girl, Valda.

Lived on the Jackson farm for two years till I was sixteen, but farming is always uncertain, so I and Jay decided we could do better if we worked at public work—that's what farmers called jobs. I worked in a flashlight battery place, two years on the night shift, but I had taught Jay how to play rhythm on an acoustic, and by then Clayton had learned bass fiddle, and so we became the Perkins Brothers Band, played weekends in honky-tonks, dodging beer bottles. First when they started fighting, we'd play extra loud, then we'd start running out through windows. Rough, man, rough—I saw a lot of blood in those places, working two, three nights a week.

35

I met Valda then and would have married her right away, but I couldn't support her, 'cause I was supporting Mom and Daddy, so I went with her four years. I married her Saturday, January 24, 1952, and on Monday I was laid off my job. Valda was a receptionist for three doctors. We moved in with my folks in Hickstown, the slum part of Jackson, had one room. Valda's money bought a bedroom suite. With her encouraging me, I decided to try and make my living singing, so I started taking jobs every night in the honky-tonks. After a year Valda wanted her own home, so I gave fifty dollars on credit for a dining room suite and we moved into a government project, Parkview Courts it was called, two rooms up, two down, concrete floors, and not even a window fan. It'd get so hot in there at night that I'd take water and sprinkle it on the bed. I was averaging thirty dollars a week then.

By 1955 I had sent tapes out. A guy there in Parkview, name of Curly Griffin, had a tape recorder. He was blind, Curly. And Fluke, that's W. S. Holland, came in then too. He used to come with me and Jay and Clayton to jobs and hit his bare hands on Clayton's bass, that was his drum. He was delivering coal then. Jay was living at Parkview too. So anyway, I made a tape in 1955 and sent it to Sun. I had sent tapes to RCA and Columbia and had never heard a thing from 'em. I had sent them to addresses from song books, like to "Columbia Records, New York City," and no other address. I called Sam two weeks later and he said, "I ain't heard it and I'm taking no auditions. I got this new boy Elvis and he's fixin' to be hot and I can't handle anymore."

I said, "Mr. Phillips, I hope someday you do hear us." 'Cause Elvis had just come out with a song, "That's Alright, Mama," and it was exactly the type of thing I was playing. I knew it would be the big time for us if Sam could hear us. Elvis, he came from the same environment as me, though not as poor, and he told me later that he had come up to Jackson and seen us one night at the El Rancho. His manager then, Bob Neal, a big DJ at WMPS in Memphis then, he had seen us too.

So I felt I had a real chance, and decided Sam Phillips was gonna hear us one way or another. A month after that, I still couldn't get over hearing the Elvis record. W. S. had a car good enough to go to Memphis, mine was a '40 Plymouth with bad tires, and we drove down to Memphis and just walked in. A secretary was saying Sam wasn't there when he walked in. I said, "I'm Carl Perkins from Jackson, sir," and he said, "No, boy, I'm not taking nobody." I said, "Just ten minutes," and he said okay I did "Turn Around" for him and he liked that. Then I did some fast things and he said that was too much like Elvis, but he liked the country material.

He recorded "Turn Around" that day and we went home. Two months went by and we kept the radio on all the time to hear it. Sam had said it would be out in a week. Then one day I was listening to Bob Neal, and he said, "We got a new song by a new artist, Carl Perkins." Valda, she dropped the baby, and I like to fainted. After that I put out "Let the Jukebox Keep on Playing" and "Gone, Gone, Gone," and then Sam sold Elvis, and he said I could record the stuff I like to do. So on December 17, 1955, I wrote "Blue Suede Shoes." Recorded it December 19, and it was released January 1, 1956.

Funny thing, it was "Honey Don't" on the back side that broke first in Memphis. Then one day the lady across the street came over and said there was a long distance call for me. It was Sam and he said, "Carl, you know what happened? You got a hit on 'Blue Suede Shoes.' Chicago has ordered 25,000. When they said that I thought they said 2,500. Never had an order so big."

So it was all happening. Then on March 22, 1956, we were on our way to do the Perry Como Show Saturday in New York, then Ed Sullivan Sunday. David Stewart, our manager and a Memphis DJ, was driving. We had played in Norfolk, Virginia, on Wednesday and were supposed to be in New York Thursday. We were near Dover, Delaware, about six-thirty in the morning. Dave was getting sleepy, was going to wake someone soon. Me and Jay were in the back seat stretched out asleep. I remember the Chesapeake Bay Ferry, and it's the last thing I remember for three days. We crashed. I broke my right shoulder in three places and four ribs and was in traction for eight days with sixteen pounds of lead to pull my neck out. Clayton and W. S. were beside my bed when I woke up in the Dover hospital. I asked what had happened then fell back asleep, but I heard a guy in the room say one of us was killed. I started screaming for a nurse, thinking Jay had died. She said Jay was alive, but our car had killed a man in a pickup we had hit, but I kept bothering her to get me moved into his room. I remember when I got moved in and saw him, Jay was asleep. I lay there watching him and waiting, and when he woke up and opened his eyes, man, we were happy boys.

"Blue Suede Shoes" was the big song in the nation then, and we were getting hundreds of letters a day telling us to get well. Valda was expecting our third child, so I talked the doctor into letting me go back home to be with my woman. And there I was one night when Elvis was on the Jackie Gleason show. He came on and said, "I want to do my new record." And he sang, "One for the money . . ." I near fell out of bed. It was "Blue Suede Shoes!"

But anyway, Elvis had the looks on me. The girls were going for him for more reasons than music. Elvis was hittin' 'em with sideburns, flashy clothes, and no ring on that finger. I had three kids. There was no way of keeping Elvis from being the man in that music. I've never felt bitter, always felt lucky being in the music business at all. Most kids from my background never drive a new car.

I started working again in September because the money was good. Jay didn't come back at first, then did for a few months, but he never really got over the wreck. He lived until October 22, 1958. Started getting headaches the January before that, then lost control of his left side. Was dying for ten months, Jay was. The last four months I quit working to be with him, took him fishing, stayed with him in general. He died holding my hand, working his mouth, I don't know what he was trying to say. Gave me his boat motor, gave Clayton his guitar. Said he'd be waitin' on us.

It's been eleven years now. I walk out to his grave and talk to him in my own way. Sometimes on stage I hear him say, "You're doing great. Jump, Carlie, jump, you got 'em jumpin'!" It was Jay and me, we were closer than me and Clayton. Clayton was the baby, but me and Jay were inseparable. Jay was big and strong. Nobody laughed at him but one time, but he was liked by everybody who ever knew him—the type of man I've strived to be.

I didn't do any work until the early part of 1959. I had spent all my money on hospital bills, and I had to go back. Then it got hard. See, I had started drinking in those honky-tonks, people would set beers up on the stage saying, "Give that Perkins boy some beer, he'll make that guitar talk." By 1959 I was

40

drinking heavy. When you're a country boy just months from the plow, and suddenly you're a star with money in your pockets, cars, women, big cities, crowds, the change is just too fast. You're the same person inside, but you're a star outside, so you don't know how to act. You're embarrassed about the way you talk, the way you eat, the way you look. You can't take the strain without a crutch. For me it was booze—I've seen the bottom of a lot of bottles.

I'd be sitting in a hotel room before going on, start thinking about Jay and how he wasn't there to be with me, and I'd get real high. I had to have it, would give fifty dollars for a pint. "Early Times" was my drink, but I'd take anything. I just floated around. Left Sam in 1959, it seemed everybody was leaving Sun, 'cause it was the dream of an artist to be on a big label. I took a chance to go with Columbia; then over there I got lost in the shuffle. On Sun I would have got more attention. I recorded regularly, but nothing would happen; good reviews but no sales. Started touring on my own, playing the Las Vegas circuit. Clayton, he was drinking heavy too, and we busted up in 1963, 'cause alcohol was making troubles. As long as W. S. was with us, he kept us apart—W. S. doesn't drink at all. But he had left us for Carl Mann. Then Johnny Cash needed a drummer; W. S. and Marshall, John's bass player, were both boat racers, and Marshall suggested W. S. and W. S. went and stayed with Johnny. Clayton is a high strung boy, always in trouble fighting with people we were working for. He loved to scrap, Clayton did, so we didn't get along.

When we busted up, I decided to quit, quit the whole business. I just stayed at home. But then we needed money, so I started work as a single, playing with anybody. I got booked on a tour—four weeks in England, me and Chuck Berry, the Animals, and the Nashville Teens. When I stepped off the plane and saw signs, "Welcome Carl Perkins, King of Rock," I said, "Lookee here, Carl, you got a place in the music business." Chuck had never been over there either and we packed the places. The kids went out of their minds, and I felt like a star. I started lightening up on the bottle, came home, and decided I was gonna make it as big as anybody.

That first trip was in 1964, the fall, and I went back two times in '65 as a headliner, star of my own show. Bad luck again late that year—shot up my foot out hunting and was out of work for months. Then one day in January, 1966, a big bus pulled up in front of my house and a big lookin' guy came up our walk. Valda called to me, "That's Johnny Cash coming up, Carlie." I hadn't seen him for three, maybe four years.

"I want you to come with me up to Nashville to play on a record," he said, and I went. Then up there he said, "I'm going to Chattanooga, Carl, and I want you to open the show," and since then I've been on every show. I'm in to stay; I'll never leave Johnny. He was my strength. It was his hand I shook and said I'd never touch the bottle again.

Johnny grew up across the river from me, and the same '37 flood he sings about in "Five Feet High and Rising" ran out over the flatlands on my side too. John and me, the similarities between us are amazing. The first real show we were on together was the first for both of us. Bob Neal booked it, and it was at Marianna, Arkansas, on a flatbed truck on a football field, thirty-five people there, and he was scared to death and so was I. One time we sat down and wrote down comparisons. He's got a lot of the same scars, he lost his brother Jack, he was hooked on pills like me on the bottle, and we got off 'em at the same time. The likenesses went on till they got so spooky we stopped comparing.

We worked with Elvis a lot, playing these little schoolyards around Arkansas and Mississippi, and I could tell you things you wouldn't believe. Back in those days, me and my two brothers and W. S., well, we were so good Elvis didn't dare go on after us. Me and my guitar playing beat his ass every time. He hadn't hit as a sex symbol then. One time in Amory, Mississippi, Johnny Cash opened the show. I was second, and they kept calling me back till I was exhausted. Elvis went on and the place emptied. A long time later, after "Blue Suede Shoes," Col. Parker wanted to book us together, and Elvis said, "I won't do it." He hadn't forgot.

No, I had no idea what we were doing down there, that music, that it would be so big. It was something to have it accepted. Like when you get a gold record, you feel you've arrived at the place you wanted to be, not down below anyone anymore. I still have mine at home and I still look at it. But I don't want to be the biggest thing in the business. I want to cut records and sell, but I want to live my life, and you can't do that when you're

number one. I want to be somewhere down on the ladder, but on the ladder.

My four children. There is Stanley, he's sixteen—I just bought him a SX Super Sport Oldsmobile; it was sitting in the driveway for him when he got home. I remember when I was sixteen I got a secondhand bicycle, and I feel like trying to make up for a few things I didn't get. Valda and I talked it over. I thought, "Maybe in a few years I'll lose him to the army," so we figured that if we treat him like a man, maybe he'll be one. He plays drums and has a little group that's real good. Debby, she's fifteen, and she plays organ; Stevie, thirteen, he's all sports, a baseball fan, but eleven-year-old Greg, he's been playing electric bass for two years and he can go! I got a room set up so we just have to flip a few switches and we can play. We make close family music. Valda plays fine piano too.

And I write songs still. I listen to practically everything people say to me and what they say to others, listening for sayings or ideas, and if there's one that stays in my mind, well, I'll be in a dressing room or at home, my guitar in my hand, and the music and words come out together. A good song, one that sells, is one that the mass of people can associate with, that says something they've felt. Or it reminds them of their childhood, or says something they'd like to do or be. The more people you can reach with your song, the better song it is, and the more likely you'll sell. A combination of good material and a lot of luck, that's what makes a song a hit, and a singer and picker a star.

The Cash Show bus rolled on through Texas. El Paso was still two hours away. The prairie was turning a dusty gold at the first beginnings of sunset, and the bus was quiet; Carl back at his Norman Vincent Peale, the others staring out the windows. Carl says he hates the road. "People'll tell you how great it is, but I won't. I do it 'cause I have to. All I'm hoping for in the world is to get to where I can close the case on that Epiphone guitar and not open it until *I* want to open it.

But they are all good old boys to their bones, and they have a fine time. The Cash Spectacular (which also includes The Tennessee Three, the Carter Family—Mother Maybelle and her daughters Anita, Helen, and June—and the Statler Brothers) tours ten to fifteen days a month. Carl, W. S., and Marshall triple up in motel rooms to save money, but otherwise it's comfortable travel-

44

ing. They talk about the old days, Elvis ("He had a project to see how many girls he could make. He did okay," said Johnny.), and sing Jimmy Rodger's songs, cracking up on each yodel; they exchange Nashville gossip, swap car and boat info, and tell jokes ("Hear about the girl who said, 'Give me nine inches and hurt me,'?" said Carl. "So the guy screwed her three times and punched her in the mouth.")

Carl's only real problem is homesickness; three days on the road and he's moaning about his "poor ole Valda" and how he can't stand being without her. He broke the silence that afternoon with just such a moan, like the howling of a Tennessee hound, that made everyone jump.

"Ooooh, where are you Valda," he cried. "D'y'know, when I call Valda, I make sure I'm at a window where I can see the moon. When I talk to her, I say, 'Valda, can you see that moon?' and she says, 'Yes, I can, Carlie, it's beautiful, isn't it,' and I say, 'Sure is, Valda,' and then our love goes from each of us, to the moon, and then to the other."

Carl paused while the others laughed. "I don't think true ladies and gentlemen would laugh at the tender outpourings of a man's heart," he said, his lantern jaw twisted with woe, and they laughed even harder.

He misses his children almost as bitterly. When he's away they often stay at his father's farm, and Carl is glad they're learning country ways. "I think the happiest time in my life was when I was a little boy in the country in the summer. Then I thought time was standing still and the world was mine." But he's finally getting things set up for Valda and the kids. They've just moved into a new house, and with Carl's drinking days behind him, they're piling up a nest egg. Johnny Cash's TV show has given him national exposure, his Sun records have been re-released, and Columbia has put out an LP of his biggest hits. Cash has had hits with several of his tunes, and Carl has high hopes for his new ballads, including a lovely song called "Constantly" that could become a pop-country standard.

"It's all in how you look at things," Carl finished, picking up *The Power of Positive Thinking* again. "I figure I went from low to high to low to just about right in the middle. That's an advance, isn't it? And maybe now I'm inching forward again."

"Poor ole Carl," said June, grinning warmly.

B. B. KING

At the end of 1969 B. B. King played the Fillmore, three years after Bill Graham first booked him and presented his blues to the young white rock fans. In those years, particularly the third, he had become prosperous and famous. Dozens of magazines had interviewed him, he had appeared on all the late night television panel shows, his albums were best sellers, and his singles were even edging into the charts. A year before when he played San Francisco he had stayed at the Oakland Holiday Inn; after the Fillmore he had done Oakland's black Club Showcase. This time he was at the Mark Hopkins, and his next date was a concert in the Hollywood Bowl. The chitlin' circuit wasn't behind him forever ("I still want to play for the people who were so loyal to me," he said), but the need to do that endless grind was over. He had made it, and was on his way to becoming what he is now, the true king, the Duke Ellington of the Blues.

He was playing and singing better than ever before, his control tighter and his emotional range wider. Where he might once have fallen back on surefire routines, he was experimenting. A year before he had said how he envied the melodic inventiveness of Charley Byrd and Kenny Burrell. "I just don't know where they get all those little notes, then string 'em together in pretty tunes," he said. "Oh, man, I'd like to play like that." At the Fillmore he was, still playing blues, but opening up their structure to a new lyricism. His singing could be no more rich than it always had been, but now it had a flamboyant zest that made him seem to sparkle in the spotlight. Most extraordinary, his process, which virtually no black entertainer over thirty is ever seen without, was gone. He looked younger, and when he smiled, he looked like a ten-year-old at a carnival. Every crowd gave him long standing ovations.

"Yes, I'm liking success, all of it," he said one night in the dressing room. "My music is getting out, and I'm not having to worry where the next dollar is coming from no more. I'm not rich, understand, but farther from the edge than ever before."

A year before I had traveled with B. B. in the deep South; there and then the edge was a lot closer.

A cool night breeze blew outside, across the Mississippi and the cane fields that press against the town of Port Allen, Louisiana. Inside the Club Streamline, a bare cinder-block box crowded with chipped, linoleum-topped cafeteria tables, it was noisy, stifling, and rank with sweat. B. B. King was an hour late. He was coming from Mobile, where he had played the night before, and the customers—field workers in collarless shirts, city dudes from Baton Rouge on the other side of the river, orange-haired beauticians, oil refinery workers with their wives—were grumbling. "We want B. B.," shouted a lady with a heavy sprinkling of gold teeth.

" 'Deed we do," answered someone, but Sonny Freeman and the Unusuals, King's six-piece touring band, kept rolling through "Eleanor Rigby." Then from a side door B. B.'s valet carried in a big red guitar, plugged it into a waiting amplifier, and left it gleaming on a chair in the dim yellow light.

"Lucille is here; B. B. can't be far behind," said the gold-toothed lady.

The tenor sax man took the mike. "Ladies and gentlemen, it's show time, and we're *happy* to pre*sent* the *star* of the *show,* the King of the *Blues,* Mr. B. B. *King.*" A wave of clapping washed back to the bar, and a heavyset man in a shiny maroon suit stepped lightly to the stage and picked up the guitar. The band started "Every Day I Have the Blues," and B. B. King, eyes screwed shut and body bent forward, hit a quick chord.

From that instant the very molecules of the air seemed alive; King and his guitar were a magic source of energy from which came fine glistening notes that drew the whole club into their tremulous, hesitant intensity. "Put the hurt on me," a man yelled. Women jumped up and stood twisting their hips, heads bowed, hands held high in witness. "Evra day, evra day I have the blues," B. B. sang, rocking back and forth, both fists clenched beside his head, and the shouting went on.

"Thank you, ladies and genulmen," King said smoothly when he finished, the band riffing gently behind him. "So sorry I'm late, but we're so glad to have you with us and we hope to he'p you have a good time. If you like the blues, I think you will. Are you ready to get in the alley?"

A deafening roar said yes. He hit a high note that bent flat as it faded, then another, then another, the crowd erupted, and he was off again. For an hour he played the blues, rough and smooth, exultant and downhearted, blues that are fresh every time: "Rock Me, Baby," "Three O'Clock Blues," "Don't Answer the Door," and his classic "Sweet Little Angel."

> *"I got a sweet little angel,*
> *I love the way she spreads her wings . . .*
> *when she puts her wings around me,*
> *oh, I get joy and everything."**

But at the break B. B. wasn't so happy. Splashing his thick neck with Fabergé Brut and touching up his roughly processed hair with Ultra Sheen, both proffered by Wilson, his valet, he moaned about his gas pains.

He's been going to a doctor for his stomach, he told the knot of hangers-on gathered around his dressing-room chair like retainers at a friendly throne, but that doctor hadn't meant nothing but misery.

" 'No fried or fatty foods,' he says, 'no salad dressing, no liquor, and no women.' I told him, I said, 'Doc, those first things maybe, even liquor, but the last, forget it.' And he said to me, 'B., you can *say* forget it, but the pills I'm givin' you for your stomach, they gonna *make* you forget it.' "

He paused to get a chuckle of appreciation from the admirers. It came, and B. B. smiled too. "I'm not through yet, lemme go on.

"Now I didn't believe that doctor that some pill was gonna make *me* forget it, and for three weeks it didn't, I was goin' just like always. And then this morning, I was with a sweet gal I been trying to make for fifteen years. She finally said the time was right, so there we was, trying to get something done before I had to get up and drive all the way here, and, you know what?

49

Wouldn't do a thing! Not a blame thing," and he slapped his thigh, laughter bubbling out of him. "I played with it, *she* played with it, but it just lay there like a hound," and he held his index finger out, limply crooked. Everyone backstage broke up with B. B., and he sat there basking in his own joke, his grin wide and loose.

He went back on stage, chuckling, this time in a light green suit, purple turtleneck, and gold pendant. It was one o'clock, late for working people on a weekday night, and the club was emptying. But King played on, oblivious of the tables deserted but for bottles and overturned glasses. "Look at him, man," said Elmore Morris, King's entr'act singer for eleven years. "The greatest. It's the depths he gets to—he knows what they are and how to get to 'em. A mean man or a small man couldn't do that; takes a real man like B. to penetrate like he does."

Born Riley B. ("I never knew what that B. was for.") King in Itta Bena, Mississippi, he became Riley King, the Blues Boy from Beale Street, when he got his first radio job in Memphis in 1948; in time that got shortened to Blues Boy King and then to B. B. "It still means Blues Boy," he says. "That's what I am. It's too late to change." Now forty-four, he looks his age but not a day older; there is no stoop in his stance, no gray in his hair, and no tiredness in his bright eyes and lively mouth. His face most often has a calmly mournful quality but can break up in laughter and suddenly have an impishness that just as suddenly disappears. At times, particularly in his Cadillac, he looks like a sober Negro doctor, exuding quiet success, but even then you see in his eyes that he is a bluesman, a man for whom the blues are his sorrow, his power, his essence. "I always start my show with 'Every Day I Have the Blues,' " he says simply, "because it's true."

The blues—"American music," says B. B.—are hard to define. "If you have to ask, you'll never know," some say, others adding more aggressively, "If you ain't got 'em, don't mess with 'em." The passion expressed in blues is, however strong, so subtle that great debates have always raged over which musicians and fans could really (or *really* really) play or feel them. Purists believe that the true bluesmen (all black) could be counted on two hands; blues democrats argue that Moses, Beethoven, Ghandi, and all disappointed lovers know the blues.

50

The evidence is on the side of the democrats. As musical form, the blues emerged less than a hundred years ago out of the peculiar institution of slavery of Africans in America; they are now a metaphor for emotions felt by people all over the globe. Blues are at the essence of a wide range of American musics, and have influenced all modern composers. Whatever the bastardized or attenuated idiom or style they get shoved into, they always maintain their integrity against depredation.

The blues are first the music of black Americans. Their technical basics evolved in the meeting of black slave and white master cultures; in time they accumulated a vast range of meanings, subjects, and styles. The blues have become the aggregate expression of black Americans, detailing every facet of their lives, reflecting every change in their fortunes, and speaking, often obliquely, their self-assertion in a world that tries to trap them in invisibility. The fundamental requirement of the blues is absolute honesty, and they are accurate to the last nuance of black life in America. Aesthetically, they *are* black America, and to love them, to find expression of oneself in them, is to identify with the black American experience.

That experience is as diverse as the blues, but its unifying fact is displacement—simply not being at home. The blues are the music of a people profoundly alienated, a people making their way in a foreign land—Babylon, Eldridge Cleaver calls it—to which they were brought as captives. On one hand attempting to deal with the cruel or absurd reality facing them as best they can, they are also searching for a surer, more essential reality—their past, their historical, racial, and primal selves, and the web from which they were ripped. One feels the earnestness of that search, its yearning and frustration, in every blues chorus with its Sisyphus-like climb away from the tonic chord, the brief reaching of an instable peak, and the inevitable fall back to the tonic.

But so powerful is the world black Americans live in that the search must be carried on within its terms. Though the blues are always played on Western instruments, the "blues scale" is not Western. The notes that give blues their emotional tonality are not the "do re mi" that white Americans call "the scale." Guitars are not fretted to include them; "blue notes" are between the keys, as pianists say. A blues musician can only reach them by distorting the sound their instruments were built for—bending a guitar string, fading open trumpet valves, "overblowing" a harmonica, or grace-noting across several piano keys. He must twist and restructure the reality he is given to find his way through to those tones that soothe and inspire him. Using the tools of the West, he over and over again recreates those haunting notes that seem to be an elusive key to a past and self remembered only well enough to make its disappearance agonizing. The tragedy of the blues is that you can't go home again; their hope is that through them, maybe someday, somehow, you can. And right now, you can make where you are a lot more homey.

The dialectic of displacement and the yearning for home is universal, a theme as old as man's expulsion from Eden and as new as our own births, yet the popularity of the blues indicates that it has particular relevance today. Did we know it no other way, the worldwide acceptance of the blues would prove that millions of men now feel robbed of their homes, cheated of their birthrights, lost and oppressed. A lot of people in this world of all colors and cultures are niggers, and they have the blues.

In a century the blues may be a form like the sonata form, something to be learned from a book. Today they are living truth. And an American one; while the world is being Americanized (i.e., accepting the technology of the white master culture), it is also (maybe therefore?) learning the other side of American life, the loneliness of displacement. Blues truth runs counter to hysterical confidence in progress, machines, and human power. It is a darker, more fateful, though ultimately more relaxed and humorous truth that has its own sober and sensual comfort. "When it all comes down," say the blues (here in the words of Memphis Slim), "you gotta go back to Mother Earth." The blues tell that truth with the ease and grace of folk tales, as well as with raunchiness, anger, and despair.

This simple music bears that truth's burden easily, because it is not quite an "art," but the vital creation of men of very human genius.

King is one of those men. He had been on the road for almost twenty years, but the day when he was a James Brown, a sex symbol with top-10 songs, has been over for a decade. Soul music, with a heavy beat, strong gospel influences, and glamorous stars, is the staple of the best-selling charts, not the blues as played by older men who won't change the rhythm to suit the latest dance steps. Blues are "roots": recognized as the basic source but ignored because they merge into the cultural background. It is the Otis Reddings, Bob Dylans, Rolling Stones, and Janis Joplins who, working changes on the blues, get the hits. Even when folk enthusiasts in the late fifties and early sixties were "discovering" blues singers like Son House and Mississippi John Hurt, B. B. was passed over as too urban and sophisticated. His blues are all music created by city artists in the past twenty years; few date directly from the oral tradition of the country blues singer. But B. B., long caught in the middle, is now getting full attention.

On one hand, educated blacks who had scorned the blues as dirty music, as an opiate of the people, and as a result of an oppressed past, are turning to them to express their blackness; B. B. is both funky enough and modern enough for them to dig. For a Negro to say, "B. B. is my main man," Charles Keil wrote in *Urban Blues,* "is to say, 'I take pride in who I am.' " On the other, the millions of white kids going deeply into rock 'n' roll, led by young white guitarists like Michael Bloomfield, Eric Clapton, and Elvin Bishop, began to discover the blues in the mid-sixties. The touted "New Rock" is as much a blues revival as it is electronic psychedelia. What the Beatles are to the latter, B. B. is to the former. For blues fans, black and white, not only is King a beautiful musician, he is the essence of the lead guitarist, the soul man alone with his guitar, a breed that for cultists has all the misterioso allure of the cowboy, racing driver, or bullfighter. Both audiences recognize him as a proud and intelligent man, an artist who presents himself with no apologies and no put-ons.

"I'm different from the old blues people," he says. "I don't smoke or drink on stage. And unlike the new ones, I don't dance. I'm just not electrifying. I figure that it's the singing and the playing the people come for and that's what I give 'em.

"My only ambition is to be one of the great blues singers and be recognized. If Frank Sinatra can be tops in his field, Nat Cole in his, Bach and Beethoven and those guys in theirs, why can't I be great and known for it in blues? It's been a long time, and the fellas that made it before me with the twist and rock, I'm not saying they don't deserve it, but, I think I do too."

In Port Allen recognition seemed a long way away. The group had just started forty-five straight one-nighters in clubs on the "chitlin' circuit" that would have them crisscrossing the Deep South. They would get good crowds because it's blues country, but they knew they'd been doing it for years and that you don't make money from people who don't have it themselves. And that night, right after the Club Streamline promoter said he didn't have the $650 promised and B. B. wearily took four hundred dollars, there was trouble.

They left the club at 3:00 A.M.—B. B., his road manager Frank Brown, and Wilson in the green Cadillac Fleetwood Brougham, the band in a Ford Econovan (a disparity exactly expressive of their business relationship to B. B.; despite it they are all friends). They planned to drive the two hundred miles to the motel in Mobile by morning, sleep until early afternoon, then drive to Montgomery for the date that night. While they gassed up in Baton Rouge, Wilson and two guys in the band walked over to a café for sandwiches. No eating at the counter, said the door attendant as a dozen white toughs watched over their beers; no takeouts either. "We're Wallaces," shouted a tough. "Great, man," sneered Wilson from the door. "Whah, you nigger," said a tough, coming out after him and punching him to the gravel. "Git 'em!" cried another, and suddenly the whites were outside, one swinging a heavy chain.

The three fought back, and when Frank, a giant, came running and grabbed away the chain, the whites scattered. But tenor sax man Lee Gatling had been stabbed in the arm and trumpeter Pat Williams was bleeding from a chain wound on the forehead. The police who gathered asked a few questions, said they couldn't find any suspects, and stood under the blue-white gas station lights eyeing the band suspiciously.

King, who had missed the action because he was in the men's room, quickly took charge, ordering the ambulance, calming his men, and talking to the police, but his mind was somewhere else. "Wanted something to eat, just something to eat and a man'll hate you so bad he'd kill you. You think things are getting better," he said to no one in particular, staring at the "I Have a Dream" stickers on his bumper. "Thought you knew how to get along, never anything like this happen before. Oh, man, this hurts so bad. And they tease me when I sing the blues. Hah! What else can I sing?"

They all waited at the hospital until six before a doctor

appeared and said Williams was all right. As the sun rose they started for Mobile, getting there, sleepless, in the glare of early afternoon.

B. B. got a few hours' sleep in before they started out for Montgomery. The anger of the night before was beginning to recede, and as the Cadillac swept north, he talked about his life. He had told his story before to other interviewers, often in the same words, as if he had saved it all up, knowing it would one day be worth telling. His mother had left his father when he was four, taking him to the Mississippi hills and her churchgoing family. She died a few years later, and he spent his boyhood as a fifteen-dollar-a-month hired hand for a white tenant farmer until his father found him and took him back to the Delta, where he chopped cotton and drove a tractor on a plantation.

He had sung in church since he was tiny and learned guitar from a minister uncle, first sneaking the guitar off the bed where the uncle put it while he ate dinner. In the Delta he started singing and playing regularly in a gospel quartet.

At eighteen he was drafted and then deferred—the plantation owners wanted good workers on the homefront—something B. B., who misses having no formal musical education, is still bitter about: "If I had been let stay in, I could have gone to music school on the G.I. Bill." But then it meant getting Army equivalent pay instead of fieldhand wages and having money in his pocket. "I'd take the extra and buy a bus ticket for as far as it would take me—Jackson, Oxford, even Hattiesburg—and play the blues on street corners, making more on a weekend than I could all week. 'Course, I was sneaking away; playing blues if you were in a sanctified singing group was evil, consorting with the devil. But I didn't mind 'cause of the money, and all those cheering me as I played, that made it worth it."

After the war he moved to Memphis, determined to make it. He lived with his cousin, the great bluesman Bukka White, and landed a ten-minute spot on WDIA, one of the first radio stations anywhere with Negro personnel, advertising Pepticon Tonic and playing his blues. He was immediately popular; by 1949 he had the best-known blues trio in Memphis, his own show as a disk jockey, and his first big record, "Three O'Clock Blues," which stayed at the No. 1 spot in the rhythm and blues charts for eighteen weeks.

"I was a star from then on, getting good guarantees, making every record—'Sweet Sixteen,' 'Rock Me, Baby,' 'You Know I Love You'—a hit. Always traveling, too. One year we did 342 one-nighters, me and Lucille," patting the guitar case behind his head. The present Lucille, a red Gibson with gold frets and mother-of-pearl inlay, is Lucille No. 7; a label on the case says, "My name is Lucille, I am a guitar. My boss is B. B. King. Please Handle Me With Care."

"Lucille got her name in a nothing town by the name of Twist, Arkansas. We were playing some club, and some guys were fightin' and they knocked over a kerosene barrel and burned the place down. I was almost killed going back in to save my guitar, and when I found out the fight was over a gal named Lucille, I named my guitar that to tell me to keep her close and treat her right."

The car slipped through miles of forest. Frank had the radio on jazz softly. . . . Harder times came in the late fifties and early sixties. When Top-40 programing swept radio everywhere, replacing specialty shows like blues hours with solid pop, B. B. didn't get much air play. Most bluesmen either moved to rock or went off the road; blues became the music of country people, the old and the poor. He always had work, but the clubs and money weren't good, especially compared to the standards set by black stars making it in white markets. He still recorded, but the albums sold for $1.99 on drugstore racks. One car crash wiped out his savings; another almost took off his right arm.

"Then my second wife left me and it like to killed me. I really loved that gal, but she wanted me off the road. I wanted to, too, but I was behind to the Government so I couldn't, but she didn't understand. Just being a blues singer was hard. People thought they were all illiterate, drinking and beating their women every Saturday night. I'd fight for the blues, but they wouldn't listen, and since I didn't have school past ninth grade I didn't feel too confident of myself. I'm still a country boy, a little scared of people who can make you feel bad. It's like since I was a boy going to bed with no lights 'cause there was no electricity, I've been afraid of the dark."

That night B. B. was magnificent. The Montgomery Elks Club, Southern Pride Lodge No. 431, was packed to the walls with a good-time crowd, and he worked for them. His face beaded with sweat, Lucille brought up under his chin, his eyebrows going up and down, B. B. pulled out the notes, starting solos with just the rhythm of organ and drums, and building slowly to the full power of the band behind him, Lucille always showing the way. When you thought Lucille had said it all, King sang, his voice both tough and vulnerable. Young white audiences marvel at his guitar playing, but for the blacks he is a blues singer, first and last. "I've been down-hearted, baby, every since the day we met," he began one song softly, ending in full-blown shouting:

> *Ah gave you a bran' new Ford,*
> *You said, "Ah wan' a Cadillac!"*

(B. B. vamping, hand on hip, as he gave the girl's response.)

> *Ah bought you a ten dollar dinner,*
> *You said,"Thanks for the snack."*
> *I let you live in my penthouse,*
> *You said it was just a shack.*
> *I gave you seven children,*
> *An' now you wanna give 'em back!·**

With that women were jumping up and down, men

*"HOW BLUE CAN YOU GET" by Leonard Feather. © by Melva Publishing Co. Used by permission of B. B. King.

rolling back in their chairs, howling at the joke of it, and B. B. finished, *"Our love is nothing but the blues, woman; baby, how blue can you get?"* Before cheering had died down he was into a slow and very funky "Don't Answer the Door," that ended in more screaming:

> *You might feel a little sick, woman,*
> *And you know you're home all alone,*
> *I don't want the doctor at my house,*
> *So you just* suffer, suffer, suffer, *till I get home,*
> *'Cause I don't want a soul at my house*
> *when I'm not home,*
> *I don't want you to answer the door*
> *for nobody, baby,*
> *When you're home and you're all alone.†*

And then the next song and the next, fast ones, slow ones, setting up moods and dissolving them for new ones; everything was real and true. "There's no signifyin' jive with B.," shouted one delirious listener, his glass held up in salute, as King went off.

"I wish they had something could measure the pressure inside a person," King said in the cramped dressing room. He spoke softly but intensely. "Like at times when you're in a strong mood, if you've been hurt bad by a gal or your best friend. It's like that when I'm playing and I know exactly what I want to play, and it's a goal I'm trying to reach, and the pressure is like a spell— oh man, I don't have the words.

"But I know this, I've never made it. I've never played what I hear inside. I get close but not there. If I did, I'd play the melody so you'd know what it was saying even if you didn't know the words. You wouldn't know when Lucille stopped and my voice began."

A beautiful woman with a wig of rust-colored curls came in. "Hello, B., how are you?" she said.

"Happy to see you, beautiful," he said with a big smile, and kissed her.

"Haven't seen you for a year, B. Are you staying over?" she said, rearranging her curls.

"No, baby, we're going to Atlanta soon as we're ready."

†"DON'T ANSWER THE DOOR" by Jimmy Johnson. © by Mercedes Music. Used by permission of B. B. King.

She looked crestfallen. They chatted a few minutes and she left. "Man," said B. B., wiping his brow. "Gonna have to do something about those pills!"

By the car the guys in the band were talking about the fight; they hadn't stopped talking about it. They couldn't figure out the why of it. Nothing like it had ever happened to any of them; its ferocity had astonished them. B. B. joined them.

"You never saw anything like it before, B.?" asked one.

Never, and he couldn't explain it for them, he said, but things are better now. You didn't stay at Holiday Inns when he started, but in black fleabags; you kept food in the car and relieved yourself beside the road. "If you had that fight a while back, you'd be in jail now. Only one thing I regret about that fight: you fellas didn't put one of them in the hospital."

"Next time, B.," said Lee.

It was a long drive to Atlanta and B. B. felt like talking. T-Bone Walker's clean sound and Elmore James's swing were his big guitar influences; church preaching for his singing. But he always loved jazz, especially Count Basie. "I just *love* to swing, man," he said, "and nobody swings like the Count." Charley Christian's guitar was an inspiration, but "the man who won my heart" was Django Reinhardt. "He had a singing guitar, gypsy Spanish, soulful. It really filled my soul."

Classical works are too long for him, but there's no music, he said, that if he listens to it, he can't see what it's getting at, even Japanese Koto music. When he retires he'd like to have a disc-jockey show again and play whatever he liked. "All music is beautiful. Man, I got twenty thousand records and I never buy ones I don't like. I even have a record of Gene Autry singing 'T. B. Blues.' He's a rich man now but there was a time when he was saying something.

"Old bluesmen, they didn't listen to anything but blues; I do and I'm more polished than them. But blues can't be too polished; they have to be raw and soulful. They started with a fella singing to you like he was telling you a story; if he kept up the tempo, he could make a chorus fifteen, even twenty bars long if he wanted to say his piece. I was like that, but when I got a band I had to stay within twelve bars to keep with the other fellas. And man, those bars went flyin' by! But blues can't be perfect. A lotta white people can't sing the blues because their

English is too good. Blues and correct English don't sound right. You gotta break the verbs for it to be blues.

"Some say the blues are backward, but I think they can he'p black people now. If something is bothering you and you got a friend, it he'ps if you can talk about it. It may not solve it, but it he'ps. You can talk about your problems in the blues and you find people have the same problems, and then you can do something. Blues' words are usually about men and women, because that's where it all starts—men do most things on account of women—but if you hear the blues, you *know* it's about a lot more."

B. B. doesn't have a home; Memphis is home base, and he has a farm there that his father lives on, but in Memphis, as elsewhere, home is the motel room he's in. The one in Atlanta looked it. Spilled over the bed, tables, floor, and sink were briefcases full of contracts, letters, unfinished songs, notes for a book to be called "How I Play the Blues," by B. B. King; an electric pan in which he makes oatmeal for his ailing stomach; a tape recorder, a tape-cassette-radio, a dozen changes of street clothes and another dozen stage outfits, books about flying (B. B. is almost qualified as a pilot), two big red volumes of "Joseph Schillinger's System of Musical Composition" from which he is learning to write his own arrangements, copies of Billboard and soul-music magazines, and empty packs of Kools. "I've been doing this a while," he said, padding around the piles in his black silk underwear. "I own an apartment building in Memphis, wouldn't mind moving in, but whites live there, and if I moved in, they'd move out and my property wouldn't be worth a thing. That's the truth."

He found what he was looking for, a sheaf of unfinished songs. "This one I've been working on. It says what I think about myself.

> '*I ain't no preacher*
> *Not trying to be no saint*
> *Because I don't get high every day*
> *Don't mean I don't take a drink.**

That's all now, but it's gonna be a song saying, I'm just B. B., take me as I am."

"Maybe soon I'll just work weekends, maybe even have a club of my own. I got four kids by various women; they're all grown and have children. Maybe I'll enjoy my grandchildren like I never had a chance to with my own. But I'll never stop playing. As long as people'll hear me, I'll keep playing."

The next date was at the Lithonia Country Club, a place at the end of a dirt-road maze twenty miles from Atlanta. "This is a real funk," said Sonny Freeman, unbelievingly. The club, a shack, was half empty, the decor made the Club Streamline look like the Stork Club: bare wooden chairs and tables, a cracked cement floor, and a stage, incongruously lined with ripped tin foil, lit by one fixed spotlight. It was a tough night; the audience seemed to like the blues but just wouldn't clap. "You know we're working hard for you," B. B. pleaded several times. Whyncha' beat your hands together for us," but all he got was desultory applause.

"Man, you see what it's been like for us all these years," he said at the break. "It's so hard when people ain't with you. But if they can't be satisfied, man, I play for my own satisfaction."

He did. Coming back on at midnight, the club even emptier than when he had begun, he played roughly, slashing his pick across the strings in harshly vibrant chords, even breaking two strings. But as he was bringing the show to a close, he changed moods. Singing in a pure falsetto, leaving the roughness behind, he made his voice all sweet pleading.

> *Worry, worry, worry;*
> *worry's all I can do,**

he sang, his head uptilted, the light glinting off the diamond B. B. ring on his left hand.

> *Worry, worry, worry;*
> *worry's all I can do.*
> *My life is so miserable, baby,*
> *and it's all on account of you.*

The riffing of the band built through the second chorus and exploded as he started the third. "Someday, baby," he sang, his voice almost squeaking, "someday, baby, someday, baby." He

---

*"WORRY, WORRY" by David Plumber and J. Taub. © by Modern Music Publishing Inc. Used by permission of B. B. King.

63

stood there, a big, powerful man on a sagging stage lost in the scrub woods of Georgia, singing to thirty people, all black, poor, middle-aged or old, a little drunk, and only a few hours away from work the next day, singing "Someday, baby," as high as he could over and over again. One knew that for every "Someday, baby" he sang, there were many somedays on his mind. Finally, he came to the last one:

> *Someday baby,*
> *when the blindman calls my name,*
> *you won't be able to hurt on me no more, woman,*
> *'cause my heart won't feel no more pain.*

He said his thank-you's, left the stage, changed, thanked the band for playing well (as he does every night), and got into the Cadillac, turning on the portable television he keeps plugged into the cigarette lighter.

"What's happening"? he asked Frank, who has been driving for him for ten years, as they pulled out.

"Another day done passed by," said Frank.

It was a fine social night backstage at the Fillmore West after a year of days passed by.

B. B.'s stomach troubles were long gone. Two lovely young women had dropped by especially to see him; a huge black man named Ernie who he had once played with in Memphis was there and had brought a fifth of scotch. B. B. sent out for some beer. Someone else was passing around a goatskin flask of red wine.

When everyone was pretty high three young blacks came to the door and shyly asked if they could enter. B. B. waved them in and offered one his seat. No, they said, they didn't want to take up his time, but they were representatives of the San Francisco State Black Students Union, and wanted to tell B. B. that they thought he was the greatest, a real soul brother who told it without any jive. He thanked them, but their manner somehow implied a "but," and he waited for them to go on.

"I hope this isn't rude," said one, "but I wanted to ask you, if it's not too personal, why you now wear your hair natural."

"I'll tell you," said B. B. "Because I'm beginning to get a feeling for who I am. I had a process for years, partly because it

64

Left to right: Buddy Guy, B. B. King, Junior Wells

was the fashion and 'cause I thought it looked good, but I always knew it wasn't quite right; it was a mask I wore to hide something. Now I don't feel I need it anymore."

Another one said it was still pretty short, but B. B. said he had it the way he wanted it. The tall thin BSU-er, whose name was Tony and who seemed to be the leader, asked if B. B. would play for the BSU. Not this trip, he said, and they'd have to wait until he was in California again, but he'd be glad to do it free. Tony didn't quite seem to trust him; B. B. said he was a man of his word; Tony looked doubtful, and then the conversation started to get a little ugly.

It was hard to tell what the students wanted. They kept needling him with questions, often all three speaking at the same time, bursting out with an impatience both nervous and angry. What was success, why did he play for whites, did he think whites understood the blues, what was the blues, did everyone have them or only black people, did he think black people had suffered more than any other race, did he believe in violence? They were at once apologetically self-abasing, acting as if their questions were unloaded, and openly antagonistic. B. B. was remarkably polite.

He knew a lot of white people who were worse off than blacks, he said, and what the students knew from books about plantation life he knew from his own life. He had walked, he reckoned, about sixty thousand miles behind a mule plowing cotton. But they cut him off before he could finish, and he pleaded in vain to speak his mind.

"You say you lived on a plantation," screamed one student, "but was your mother and wife raped before your eyes?"

"You know they weren't because I'm still alive," said B. B.," and that would only happen over my dead body."

"But *that's* the blues," shouted another student, "and that never happened to no white man."

"You come here to ask me about the blues, and then you tell me what they are?" B. B. asked in disbelief.

"But how can you really have 'em if you say anybody can have 'em?" said Tony.

"I didn't say anybody, I just said no race got a monopoly on suffering," said B. B.

They continued at an impasse for twenty minutes, a strange spectacle: young men whose own sense of pride and dignity as humans and blacks had in large measure been awakened by B. B.'s artistry having to reinforce that still shaky confidence by attacking him. Finally they were almost calling him an Uncle Tom. For the first time, he showed anger.

"Listen," he said. "I've got only one more thing to say. You're upset now, but it don't bother me. You know a lot more about who you are than I did at your age, and I'm proud of you. You are going to be leaders and we need leaders. But there's one word I don't want you to forget, and that's justice. Be just. *Please* be just. That's the lesson of suffering and it's the lesson of the blues. I try to be just when I play my song, and if you can't be just, *that's* when you don't really know the blues."

"But, but," Tony started to stammer.

"No buts," said B. B. "Now let's shake hands and don't bother me no more."

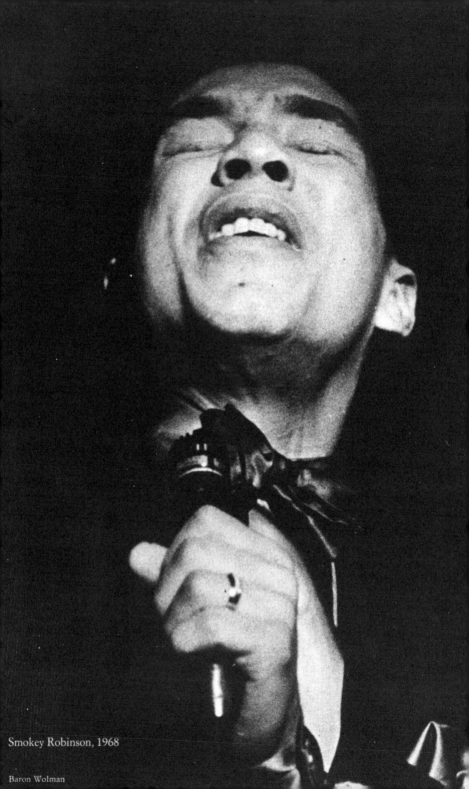

Smokey Robinson, 1968

Baron Wolman

Smokey Robinson*

Smokey Robinson stood very still in his Gucci slippers, the putter in his hand poised to swing. The first four Titleists he had tapped toward the table leg of his motel room had gone astray, each depressingly curling toward the wastebasket. The last sat innocently an inch from his right toe on the sea-green carpet. He swung, click, and away it rolled, straight for its imitation walnut goal against which it bumped, then nuzzled, at rest again.

Smokey smiled and came over to collect all five balls. He was wearing cream-colored, woolen boucle bell bottoms and a T-shirt; his short, nappy hair still wet from his 4:00 P.M. wake-up shower. An attaché case neatly stacked with papers lay open on the bed; the closet was crowded with his show suits of sateen and mohair. New Motown records—Stevie Wonder, Martha and the Vandellas, Marvin Gaye—that had been sent out to him from Detroit were scattered on the desk. Included was his own latest record, *What Love Has Joined Together,* and proof copies of its cover. The front was an informally posed color shot of himself and the three other Miracles, the back a stunning picture of Claudette, the fifth Miracle and Smokey's wife. He liked it but had just called Motown to ask for another proof with different lettering.

"See, it's gonna be a fold-out cover," he said, nudging the balls back to his shooting spot, "so I want the 'Joined Together' to be over Claudette and the 'What Love Has' over us with dots inbetween. I want to get it across that love *has* joined us together, Claudette and me and the whole group, and that love is what could join us all together."

He had the Titleists back and he went to putt again. Smokey was working on his game; putting was nice relaxation on

*Editor's Note: Originally, this article was planned to contain examples of lyrics by Smokey Robinson. Unfortunately, we were unable to arrange satisfactory terms for their inclusion.

the road—afternoon TV palls for every traveling musician—but it was real practice as well. He squirmed his feet backwards and forwards to get his weight properly balanced, checked the tilt of his head, and watched the arc made by his straight left arm as he followed through.

The first ball was dead on target. He stepped to the second; so was that. Happy, he did a hop to the third; dead on again. He was a good putter. Each shot was an almost imperceptible action, yet his grace was unmistakable. On stage Smokey looks small; agile and light-skinned, his physical presence is the opposite of the late Otis Redding's. His impulsively friendly grin and easy voice suggest a stripling of twenty, albeit a sophisticated one. As with many dancers and athletes, however, that seductive smoothness conceals a sinuously muscular power. The putter was a wand in his hands, his shoulders padded like a swimmer's.

"You heard the new record?" he asked when his putting was done, turning on the expensive portable player set up by the window closed against a sunny San Francisco afternoon. From the first notes it was unmistakably the Miracles: the impeccably muted brass and string arrangements framing the harmonizing voices, the bass and drums establishing a sure rhythm pulse, and Smokey's high floating voice leading it all to tell another tenderly melodic tale of love. But something had changed. The sound was still as lovely as ever, as bewitchingly convincing, but lusher, more sophisticated, more romantic.

"This album represents a conscious change for me," Smokey said, "It's the kind of an album I hope a guy will put on when he's alone with his girl. Our other albums were always built around singles, but this I'd call a concept album."

Song blended into song; the tempos and moods varied less than on previous records (All the songs are related to "the theme of the power of love," Smokey said.), and in places he had overdubbed the Miracles' voices to get the cushioned effect of a full chorus. The songs were longer, too, five or six minutes instead of the tight two-to-three minutes allowed the standard single. But, most important, an intensity was missing; however sweet and apparently limpid, Smokey's music had always before been bursting with immediacy, a zest just barely kept under control on the ballads and totally free on his dance numbers. In fact there was no

Smokey tune that wasn't danceable, but *What Love Has Joined Together* was, the composer had just admitted, smooching music.

The record player clicked off. Smokey sat on the bed, wrapping himself in a red woolen bathrobe, and waited, smiling, for the next question. Berry Gordy, Motown's founder and Smokey's closest friend, had just moved to Los Angeles; would Smokey move out to the Coast from Detroit too? For an instant he was wary, then effusively vague again. He wasn't sure; maybe. "Love Detroit, lived there all my life, but . . . it's out of the way, y'know? . . . You gotta admit that there's more talent, better studios, more *opportunities* in LA." He had, he said, no immediate moving plans; since the group had cut touring down to a few weeks a year, he has become more involved in the company, watching Detroit for Berry who has been setting up new operations in Los Angeles.

"I could go a lot of directions, man," Smokey said. "Y'know, the last few nights at the club people have been asking for some of our old songs, stuff I had forgotten we did, and it made me think back over the past thirteen years we've been working. We never knew where we were going and still don't, dig? Our only idea was pleasing the people, making music people want to hear. When we get those requests, I believe we did, and it makes me very happy, man, very happy."

Smokey (William is his name; intimates call him Smoke) is what MC's used to be proud to announce as an "all 'round entertainer." As good a singer, songwriter, and producer as Sam Cooke, Paul McCartney, and George Martin combined, Smokey does them all with a special grace. Plus the cautious maturity of a go-getter executive: at thirty, Smokey is also the vice-president of a multimillion dollar (and still growing) entertainment corporation, Tamla Motown Inc. By doing everything but the other vocal and instrumental parts, Smokey has a control over all stages of his art unrivaled by any other leading artist in rock 'n' roll. What the Beatles hoped to get with Apple—a self-running company, overseen by them, in which they can do and grow as they please artistically—Smokey has in Motown. He has it because he was for a decade the reigning genius of the Top-40.

By the late fifties even the toughest show business cynics had stopped saying rock 'n' roll was a fad. Five years after

71

Elvis, "teen music" was big business and a recognized segment of the music industry. Though much of the original musical energy had run down, the systems of making salable music and getting it sold were being perfected. Highly individual performers like Little Richard and other early stars were moved to the side by "groups" who had a "sound" and an "image." Inside all of those group sounds were many fine singers, but the audience wasn't supposed to know that (the singers weren't encouraged to believe it either). It was the heyday of the writer or producer—often a one-man packager—with the magical attribute of "teen feel." Some packaged commercial junk, though even much of that was brilliant, like Jimmy Drake's Nervous Norvous records; some packaged commercial art. The best were in New York, and the best in New York were producer-writer Phil Spector, and the trio of songwriting (also producing) teams: Barry Mann and Cynthia Weil, Jerry Leiber and Mike Stoller, and Jerry Goffin and Carole King.

The 45-record was their medium; the disc itself was the work of art and the end product of many processes, of which the musical performance was only one. Radio—by then as packaged as the music—was their second medium and they mastered it (payola helped, of course). They knew how to construct two minutes and fifteen seconds of song that would triumph over the DJ's blaring introduction and the pimple cream ad that chopped off the end, and still so excite a fifteen-year-old girl that she would make it a radio request, buy it and the follow-up album (the single plus ten throwaway tracks), and get it on the charts.

That was (and is) Top-40—a low stakes-high potential game for competitive perfectionists dedicated to the art and science of hitmaking. With a few hundred bucks, a little studio time and someone to sing, plus a lawyer to set you up as a company, you could have a record out on your own label, and maybe it would sell a million. Anyone could play.

One who did was Berry Gordy Jr., a very sharp cat around the rhythm and blues scene in Detroit. He had done a little of everything (including coauthor "Money," which states, quite frankly, "Money, that's what I want"), but he was determined to break out of the black performance end of the business and into the white financial end. By 1957 he was an independent producer, doing his own sessions and leasing (in effect, selling) the tapes to major labels to press and distribute. To move

Smokey Robinson, 1968

from that precarious fringe position, however, he needed a group, any five reliable and hungry black high-school kids who could do a reasonable approximation of Frankie Lymon. He took to hanging around other producers' auditions.

"One afternoon we were auditioning for some cat," Smokey recalls, "and he dug us, but wanted me and Claudette (she's my wife now) to sing in front like Mickey and Sylvia, who were big at the time. That wasn't our style. As we were going out, a guy called us over and asked to look at our songs. It was Berry—we had heard of him because he was hot, writing songs for people like Etta James and Jackie Wilson. We had a book of about a hundred songs I had written, and he liked only one, but he didn't say the rest were garbage. I must have gone through sixty-eight of those songs with Berry that afternoon, and on everyone I'd say, 'What's wrong with this one?' and he'd say, 'Well, you left off this or you didn't complete your idea on that.' That was what started me thinking about songs and what they were."

Berry started the group doing background vocals, but that was big time for the kids who by then had been the Miracles for three years. "When we got together first in about the seventh grade we didn't dream of ever being performers. We were just part of the biggest recreational thing going on in our neighborhood, man—groups. There were five on my block alone. First we were Ronnie White, Pete Moore, and myself, and then we met Bobby Rogers and Claudette. There was another cat who left after a little while; otherwise there have been no changes in sixteen years. We used to sing anywhere, home after school, at parties, sometimes whole bunches of groups would get together for singing battles. Twelve-year-old kids carrying on with music—I'm sure it's been going on since the beginning of time."

The Spaniels, the Moonglows, Dominoes, Drifters, and Penguins were their idols. Smokey's mother had a lot of Inkspots records, and he heard the blues and gospel all around him (the Reverend C. L. Franklin and his daughter Aretha were neighbors), but all that was grown-up music for Saturday nights and Sunday mornings. Smokey's father was a city employee with soberly bourgeois leanings; he strongly disapproved when his son quit junior college for show biz. As a child, protected by his family's genteel poverty, Smokey was able to be more like an All-American Boy than almost any other black artist before him. He dug the ballads of popular radio, and the first music that he bought was hit parade songbooks from Woolworth's.

To Smokey, Gordy is "the cat who really helped me get my thing together. Even after we met him, I was going to college, Highland Park Junior College, studying to be an electrical engineer. It seemed like something to *do*, dig, something that would *benefit* me. Man, I had even thought of being a dentist; I checked it out in high school but didn't dig it. I didn't know I could make it in music; Berry showed me how." A greater debt, perhaps, is owed the other way. After their very first records together (which appeared on the Chess and VJ labels), Smokey concentrated on making the music and Berry on selling it. The money from Smokey's first solid successes like "Got a Job" and "Bad Girl" (good copies of then current smashes) started Motown in 1959. The company's first hit was a Smokey and the Miracles number, "Way Over There," and it was "Shop Around," a 1961 million-seller that put the company on its feet and on the map as an important independent.

And one with a distinctive sound. Detroit may have been the boondocks, but New York was tired and claustrophobic. By the early sixties the packagers in Tin Pan Alley's Brill Building were reworking gimmicks that were refinements of earlier gimmicks. Not only did Motown have a city to itself to find talent in, but also, being black run, was a magnet for artists who felt more at home there. It was, Smokey insists, "one big happy family," and its growing stable of singers and writers and arrangers competed with and inspired each other. At first the music was primitive; instead of the strings, big bands, and complex tracking available later, Smokey and Berry were lucky to have a sax or piano with the rhythm section. Yet the Motown Sound always had a fresh and earnest excitement; a little more soulful than rock, it kept the ballad feeling of straight pop. It was, in fact, a synthesis as original as the blues-country one that started rock: the old standard sung like gospel with a rock-rhythm and blues beat. Its appeal crossed race lines and worked even beyond the pure teen market; it was, as the record labels soon proclaimed, "The Sound of Young America."

The Motown Sound was a true synthesis, not just the soft-pedaling of soul as its detractors claimed; yet in reaching so far for the ballad feel, Motown did risk losing connection with the downhome vitality that could give even the sweetest records their funky bottom. The dilemma was not their's alone; it was no accident that the Urban League and the NAACP showered Motown with distinctions, or that *Ebony* (and *Fortune*) wrote up the company as a fine example of social progress. Smokey and Berry were of the first generation of professional black executives whose way was opened by the liberal progress and affluence of the fifties. The radically anticapitalist and explicitly black consciousness that superceded "integration" and "civil rights" arrived only in the sixties when they were already millionaires. By the time the "hippie revolution" hit the world and the pop music business, they had the Supremes endorsing Hubert Humphrey and the Four Tops playing the Copacabana. Which is why Smokey, though just barely separated by age, is light-years away from artists as varied as Sly Stone, the Beach Boys, and the Kinks, all of whom owe him a great musical debt.

But musically Motown lost its groove very seldom, balancing the gooey excesses of the Supremes with the raw power of Gladys Knight. The roster of its talent includes some of the best and biggest stars of the past decade—Mary Wells, Marvin Gaye, the Supremes, The Temptations, the Four Tops, Jr. Walker, and Stevie Wonder—and dozens and dozens of its best songs by writers like the Holland-Dozier-Holland team and William Stevenson. Smokey outdistances them all. By now he has no idea how many songs he has written, collaborated on, produced, or performed himself. Some he considers duds ("I Like It Like That" is his own least favorite), but most have been sure hits. There's no formula, but each has a strong beat backed with a confidently bounding bass line, and then a seductively harmonized melody whose turns are exactly matched by the lyric's mood. All have a certain liquid elegance; Smokey makes it look easy.

Bob Dylan (press releases say) has said that Smokey is "today's greatest living American poet." Later he said he meant Rimbaud, but take "I Second That Emotion". . . .

John Lennon thought enough of the "I'm Crying" refrain in the sweet "Ooh, Baby," to cop it for "I Am the Walrus." Smokey can play gracefully with words and their repetition, or he can get right downhome and basic as in "You're My Remedy," which he did for the Marvelettes.

76

The Miracles, 1965

While his later songs have a smooth sophistication, his early songs were right in the fifties-early sixties' teen groove. "Shop Around" defines the form.

"Tracks of My Tears" is perhaps his best song; fully aware of all its elements, Smokey integrates them into a captivating whole. Marvin Tarplin, the Miracles' accompanist for years, starts it with a simple guitar riff (the idea on which Smokey based the song). The riff is picked up by the bass, and then gently accented by the drums. The group comes in with a few bars of whispered "too doo oh's," which frame Smokey as he sings alone. By then the background has built behind him, and Smokey powers out into the verse: . . . (sudden smash on the drums) . . . (another smash) . . . (and the group is now singing the ends of the lines as refrains). The tension drops immediately, only to rise higher again, fall back again, and then build to a climax when Smokey's voice is riding high over an incredible sweep of music, throwing in *"oooh's," "baby-baby-baby's"* and *"yeah's"* until there is nothing left except a fadeout as smooth as nightfall.

Tarplin's riff came to him one afternoon fooling around at home, but after he played it to Smokey, it took Smokey two months of snatched moments on planes and long rehearsals with the full group to construct all of "Tracks." "It was a lot of work getting that one in the pocket," Smokey said, "but when we did have it down, we took it into the studio and did it, doing three other tunes that session too."

To do "Tracks" and three other songs in an afternoon is to be an absolute professional; by that time, the midsixties, Smokey had arrived as a consummate Top-40 hitmaker. The Beatles, the Rolling Stones, and Otis Redding had all covered his tunes, the Miracles had been a top group for six years, and the songs kept flowing out.

They still are. The days of Top-40 dominance over rock and roll are over; the FM stations and the hip community grapevine have a hit parade of their own from which Top-40 stations take many of their cues. But Smokey's songs still glide to the Top-10. At some point the Miracles became "Smokey Robinson and the Miracles," yet neither he nor they have become stars; their personal and musical style is so self-effacing as to be almost anonymous. Fans who chase down every detail of the lives of the superstars take Smokey's gems for granted. You never have to know that it's the Miracles: a song comes on the car radio and makes you smile. You turn the volume up and start tapping the wheel; by the end you're pounding on the dash and singing along, and you feel *good*.

The night before, working at a San Francisco nightclub, Smokey had been all excitement. "I do believe that everybody wants to be loved," he had shouted out into the dark; a scattered chorus of "yeahs" came back from the crowd.

"Do you want to be loved tonight?"—this to a teen-ager with his prom-night date in the front row.

"Maybe," said the kid, embarrassed.

"Maybe?" laughed Smokey. A mischievous smile crinkled up his face. "Maybe ain't gonna get you love, you gotta want it, you gotta need it, you gotta *give* it, like this . . ." and he broke into "I'll Be There," the band taking the tempo from his snapping fingers and coming in right on time. The Miracles, in matching but slightly more subdued suits of purple mohair, swayed around their own microphone. Smokey was the center, and he held it, moving smoothly from song to song, emoting, joking, dancing, and romancing the whole club with his energy.

It wasn't the best night he had ever had. The group has almost retired from the road, and their act was a little rusty. The club was a Broadway clip joint, the stage as small and cramped as the crowd. At moments the veneer of entertainment wore thin, and the mechanics that produced the magic effects were all too obvious. But Smokey ignored the squeaking speakers and the laboring local band. For a while the show became "Do Your Thing Night," and he called up girls from the audience to sing and dance; then he got everyone to join in on "The Age of Aquarius." Smokey was working hard to please, and by the second encore of "Oooh Baby" the rough spots were gone. The whole group bowed low to take the applause as the last chord faded away, then came up smiling and waving and were off. Meaty looking ushers started clearing the tiny tables for the second show.

Now the putter stood in a corner ignored; Smokey was pacing around the motel room talking music and show biz with the same enthusiasm he had had on stage.

"I'll tell you something, man; I don't think I'd still be in this business if it wasn't for the Miracles. We've stayed together because we legitimately love each other. In some groups, everything becomes more important to the group than the members of it. You see groups of cats and they're falling out about some girl or money or this and that. It's a drag.

"Staying together has a lot to do with the way you treat people and the simple aspect of being lucky that people dig you for that long—because people don't have to dig you. This is one thing that recording artists get off into where after they've had a few hit records they think it's them. They think, 'Well, if I was the milkman, when I was coming down the street all the girls would come out of the house and say "Oh, he's coming with the milk," and tear their clothes off.'

"That's not true, man, it just comes along with the business. When you can no longer accept the fact that you're a human being and singing is just your job and along with the glamour part of entertainment comes the screams and the yells, then you're in trouble. But we want everybody to know we thank them because they've been so wonderful down through the years."

His sincerity (mentioned prominently in all Motown press releases) was a bit hard to take, but it seemed to be Smokey all the way down. With Smokey everything is "great": Henry Mancini, Burt Bacharach, Otis Redding, baseball, basketball, and music of every variety. He is mildly condescending about what he still calls the "psychedelic fad," but loves Bob Dylan and the Beatles. Dylan is "a cat who's writing the real of what he sees," and John Lennon and Paul McCartney are "two of the greatest songwriters ever. Any time you have good writers in your own group, you're bound to be big. Some of their things, like that 'I Am the Walrus' tune, I didn't understand, but with all the weird stuff they had going in it, whew, it was powerful."

His own theory of songwriting is simple: "Make a tune that has a complete idea and tells a story in the time allotted for a record. It has to be something that means something, not just a bunch of words on music. But I can write about anything. Some people say they write from experience. Not me. I can never remember having something happen and writing a song about it. I write songs no matter what mood I'm in; it's my work, dig?

"A lot of the things you hear by us, we had to splice down for radio time. Like 'Second that Emotion.' It was 3:15 when it was done and Berry—who has an ingenious sense of

The Miracles, 1968

knowing hit records—it's uncanny—he heard it, he told us, 'It's a great tune, but it's too long, so I want you to cut that other verse down and come right out of the solo and go back into the chorus and on out.' So we did and the record was a smash. He's done that on quite a few records and he's usually right, man."

He shrugged off the suggestion that maybe the song as song would have been better full-length. "No, man, I've just geared myself to radio time. The shorter a record is nowadays, the more it is going to be played. This is a key thing in radio time, you dig. If you have a record that's 2:15 long it's definitely gonna get more play than one that's 3:15, *at first*, when it's released, which is *very* important for its impact and sales.

"But it's no hangup because I'm going to work in it and say whatever I'm going to say in this time limit. It would be a hangup if I wrote five minutes of a song and then had to cut it up. But cutting thirty seconds or a minute doesn't make that much difference."

He was not aware that for many people in rock 'n' roll, the Top-40 has become an irrelevant concern. "I think that anybody who records somebody approaches it with the thought in mind that these people can be a smash. I don't think anybody thinks, 'Oh, they'll never be a Top-40 act, but here, let's record them and not be in the Top-40.' Everybody who approaches this, approaches it with the idea of being in the Top Ten because it's the only way to stay in business, and let's face it, this is the record *industry*, one of the biggest industries going nowadays.

"So we're just going to try to stay abreast of what's on the market. This is what hangs a lot of jazz musicians up. I've seen cats in little clubs who are jazz musicians through and through. They would not play a note of rock 'n' roll ever. Nothing. And they're starving to death.

"Now this gets to the point of ridiculousness to me. I don't think that they love jazz anymore than I love what I'm doing, but it just so happens that right now what I'm doing is more in demand than jazz. But you can believe if it came to a point whereas jazz was what was happening and nobody was buying this type of music and I was starving to death, I'm sure I'd write some jazz songs.

"The market, man, the market is people. It is the kids who are buying the records. This is the people you're trying to reach. I think that satisfying people on the whole if you're in business is more important that self-satisfaction."

The interview was beginning to bore him, and he frowned for the first time. It showed his age, ten years of hard work away from when he was the boy in the "nice boy next door" image he can still project on stage.

"Dig," he said, "it's like the new album we were talking about. It's just one album. If it's successful, I'll probably do another. Or maybe I'll be on the Coast with Berry working on building the business. I'll keep writing songs, but I don't see getting far out, no."

There was time for one last question. A few teen-age girls had been knocking at the door ("They oughta go down to the Fillmore if they want that," he said), and he wanted to get dressed and leave before they came back. Did he have a side of himself that demanded satisfaction free from the limits of industry and market? "I'm not sure I know what you mean," he said. "I could go into the studio and record a tune that's thirty minutes long if I wanted to satisfy my personal thing. I could record a tune that's longer than an LP, just record it, have a disc made, take it home, sit back, and dig it. But, you know, I don't think I would. If some cat did, man, great. But I wouldn't do something like that."

Janis Joplin, 1969   David Gahr

Janis Joplin

[As this book was in its final stages Janis Joplin died. Hopefully she was the last victim of the star hysteria that cruelly imprisoned many of its greatest artists in the 1960s. She was a beautiful woman.]

In the miserably rainy San Francisco winter of 1969, the late Janis Joplin was, by all the rules of show-biz myth, At a Truly Crucial Point in a Star's Career. As lead singer with the freak rock-blues group, Big Brother and the Holding Company, riding the wave of music out of the whole hip movement, Janis had become the biggest female star of rock 'n' roll. Yet a month before, with her fame still growing, she had quit to go solo and sing heavier rhythm and blues.

Within a month she would be starting the first tour with the new band. The money would be better than with Big Brother, well into five figures for most dates; her name alone, Janis Joplin, would have top billing. Would the great fan hordes, even those who felt personally betrayed when she quit Big Brother, hang with her? Would they dig what she was doing? Could she do it? The questions were hanging in the air like rain, possible to ignore, but persistently annoying.

Lit by the bright lights of the pool table, Janis was resplendent. Her wild brown hair, touched with gold, hung in untamed waves down her back and over her lavender silk shirt and blue velvet vest. Gold sandals and bright blue stockings were on her feet, on her wrists dozens of bracelets in flaming acrylic colors; a blue and red kerchief was tied loosely into her immense fur hat; silver Indian bell rings were on every finger, and she was laughing, dancing, and singing, her eyes, mouth, and body never still.

It was late afternoon in a San Francisco Irish bar, the B&G Club, and Janis was grooving. The night before she had been "feeling oh so *good* with this beautiful cat." An afternoon of drinking sweet vermouth in deep tumblers full of ice had put her in a zingy-mellow mood, and right then she was playing eight ball with a little tattooed guy, and all the luck was coming her way.

"Shoot easy, girl, and you'll either make it or leave him stuck," suggested a gaunt old barfly.

Janis, once (she says proudly) "eight-ball champion of 6th Street in New York between Avenue A and 1st Avenue," looked over the table with a practiced eye, her face set and deadly serious. With a sharp tug at the pink ribbon that belted her skin-tight purple bell-bottoms, she bent to shoot.

"Oh, no, man, I don't play like that; being that chicken-shit is tacky, man," she said and blasted away. The shot she wanted missed, but out of the clattering rebounds, the six ball dribbled into a side pocket. "MMEEEEE-OOH!" she cried, giving a quick shimmy with the cue stick high over her head, then spinning to the bar for a long gulp of her double vermouth. "I told ya, I told ya," she cackled with a grin that almost closed her eyes.

Everyone in the bar roared with laughter, even the guys in her band. Rehearsal should have started a half hour before, but the bar, unlike the dank practice room in a warehouse attic next door, was warm, and Janis was a pleasure to watch.

Bammo went the four ball. Click-zizz-clunk went the two; only the eight left. Janis chalked her cue with nonchalance.

"The side, girl, the side," whispered the barfly.

"Eight ball in the corner," she called and, pushing her bracelets up to her elbow, shot, missed by inches. "Oh, day-um," she said with a good Texas diphthong, instantly forlorn. But the little guy missed, too, and with her glee fully replenished, Janis finished off the game with a lightning stroke. "Too much," she crowed. Knocking back her drink, she slipped inside her massive Russian lynx fur coat and announced, "Okay, boys, let's go re-hearse."

"Pep," said the barfly, lifting his glass in tribute, "that girl sure has pep."

At rehearsal, the groove started to go. It took ten minutes for everybody to get there, another fifteen to get down to work, and even then things were a little too loose.

"Will you guys for Chrissakes stop moving around and talking when I'm singing?" Janis shouted in fury, breaking off the song mid-chorus.

The band stopped and watched her warily. "Hey, Janis, calm . . ." one of the musicians began.

"Calm? Listen, man, when I'm out there singing, I'm the one, right? I don't need you guys upstaging. It's my act, man, I'm the one they paid to see, dig?"

"Janis, oh Janis, we promise to be good boys," said the drummer with a broadly mock mollification that made her laugh.

"Okay, man, I'm sorry, too. I don't wanna be a bitch about it. But y'know, we got three"—she held up three fingers— "three weeks before we open in New York, and we don't have one tune really down." But the tension was seeping out. "Let's start from the top." Her voice was a bit weary.

"She's doing the hardest thing you can do—carrying a whole band on her shoulders, all the personalities, plus doing her own thing. But it's worth it. The benefits are mystical; it's a compulsion, nothing to do with reason, logic. See, first and foremost, Janis is a blues singer. Think what that means, really think. The tradition of hardship, tragedy, early death. Bessie Smith. Robert Johnson died at twenty-one. A blues singer isn't a performer, doesn't need an audience. Can sing to the ocean, the moon. Even when there are 10,000 people out there, there still might be no audience. But the blues sustain you. Blues are a faith in beauty and peace, coupled with extreme worldly knowledge; the ultimate decision is always positive." (Blues guitarist-singer-producer Nick Gravenites, and Janis's friend.)

"Oh, yeah, I'm scared," Janis had said earlier that afternoon. "I think, 'Oh, it's so close, can I make it?' If I fail, I'll fail in front of the whole world. If I miss, I'll never have a second chance on nothing. But I gotta risk it. I never hold back, man. I'm always on the outer limits of probability."

She put down her drink and pointed to a newspaper clipping on her kitchen wall, her answer to a reporter who stopped her one day to ask, "What are you doing with life?" "Getting stoned, staying happy, and having a good time," her answer read. "I'm doing just what I want with my life, enjoying it. I don't think you can ask more of life than that."

Janis Joplin, Newport, 1968   David Gahr

"My credo," Janis said laughing and looking suddenly like a little girl. "When I get scared and worried, I tell myself, 'Janis, just have a good time.' So I juice up real good and that's just what I have."

> I once had a daddy, he said he'd give me
> everything in sight,
> I once had a daddy, he said he'd give me
> everything in sight,
> So I said, honey, I want the sunshine, yeah,
> an' take the stars out of the night.
>
> —"Turtle Blues"

Go after good times, and you'll have some real bad ones; but for Janis, anything is better than a life of average ones, all the peaks cautiously leveled out for stability and longevity. "I have to be incredibly *there,* man. Whatever I do, I do a lot, and whatever it is, it's a damn sight better than being bored. Took a vacation when I thought it would be nice to do nothing after the road—man, I just about went out of my head.

"Yeah, I know I might be going too fast. That's what a doctor said. He looked at me and said my liver is a little big, swollen, y'know. Got all melodramatic—'what's a good talented girl doing with yourself' and all that blah. I don't go back to him anymore. Man, I'd rather have ten years of superhypermost than live to be seventy by sitting in some goddam chair watching TV. Right now is where you are, how can you wait?"

Janis—such a strange, unsettled mix of defiance and hesitancy, vulnerability and strength—doesn't wait; every moment she is what she feels, mean or loving, up or down, stone sober or drunk out of her skull. The intensity makes her always magical, and makes radiant her unpretty face, with its too big nose, too wide mouth, and rough complexion. She consumes vast quantities of energy from some well inside herself that she believes is bottomless, and the heat of it warms everyone who meets her. When she sings all that terrible energy is brutally compressed into the moment.

She sings jumping and dancing, her fists alternately clenching and breaking open to clap; the corners of her marvelous

*"TURTLE BLUES," words and music by Janis Joplin. Copyright © 1968 Cheap Thrills Music, 75 East 55th Street, New York, N.Y. Used by permission.

mouth turning down in the fierceness of joy breaking through anguish; her hair covering her eyes until swept back with a meaty hand. In great shouts that send her strings of beads flying and knot her face into grimaces, the energy explodes and explodes again, sending out waves of electrical excitement. Some say she can sing more than one note at a time; maybe, but does it matter? In every note there are infinite meanings.

Janis is a rock 'n' roll woman, perhaps the greatest that ever lived. There have been great woman singers of rock 'n' roll, but only a few have dared take full place in the essentially masculine world of rock stardom. Diana Ross, Martha of the Vandellas, Grace Slick, Tracy Nelson, and even Aretha Franklin are in the end female singers in the long "chantoosie" tradition; they can sing tough if they want to, but they never risk losing their essential femininity on or off stage. But Janis and a few of her sisters—Etta James, Little Eva, Sugar Pie DeSanto, Gladys Knight, and of course Big Mama Willie Mae Thornton (no one else white comes to mind except Mae West, a fine blues singer herself)—express their woman-ness with a raunchy boldness that is magnificently sexy though not one bit ladylike. Janis is a girl who has always wanted to be one of the guys, though she has always known she is a woman, and a tender one, inside. She has a masculine scorn for the politely devious wiles of acceptable femininity, yet losing a good man can break her heart. The ambiguity of brashness and softness is at the heart of her appeal; on stage, second to second, she is one and then the other, so you first glory in her strength and then want to reach out and soothe her sorrow.

Her almost inhuman devotion to the exploration of the moment has made her not just a star, but the inamorata, the "shaman mama" (said West magazine) of the hip-rock generation. She is not the symbol of its philosophy, but the thing itself: everything comes to those who don't wait. For the millions of kids who know that *NOW* is more important than the deferred gratification their parents and The System are pushing, Janis is the *belle* ideal.

"Everybody I know," Janis says, "what they're good at is being themselves. I've been doing it for twenty-six years, and all the people who were trying to compromise me are now coming to me, man. You better not compromise yourself, it's all you've got. And you don't have to, I'm a goddam living example of that.

Janis Joplin, summer, 1967, after Monterey   Baron Wolman

Janis Joplin, December 1968, after the breakup of Big Brother   Baron Wolman

"People aren't supposed to be like me, sing like me, ball like me, drink like me, live like me; but now they're paying me $50,000 a year for me to be like me. That's what I hope I mean to those kids out there. After they see me, when their mothers are feeding them all that cashmere sweater and girdle bullshit, maybe they'll have second thoughts—that they can be themselves and win. You just have to start thinking that way, being that righteous with yourself, and you've won already."

Janis has won big—not everyone trying to be themselves ends up a rock star—but it hasn't been luck. Sustaining the confidence to keep upright and moving without the support of patterned respectability demands a mixture of selfishness, cynicism, faith, and desperate yearning. Janis has them all, plus a rock-bottom toughness. Her toughness scares her; sometimes she'd give it all up to get the cozy love and life sweet girls get, but the time for that is long since past. "I guess it's lucky people like me as I am," she said, briefly disconsolate. "If they didn't, I wouldn't know how to change."

> I guess I'm just like a turtle, hiding underneath its
> horny shell,
> I guess I'm just like a turtle, hiding underneath its
> horny shell,
> But you know I'm very well protected, I know this
> goddam life too well.

Oldest child of a refinery executive in the Gulf town of Port Arthur, she's a Texas girl not cut out for Texas. "I always wanted to be an artist, whatever that was, like other chicks want to be stewardesses. Port Arthur people thought I was a beatnik, and they didn't like beatniks, though they'd never seen one and neither had I. I read, I painted, I thought, I didn't hate niggers. There was nobody like me in Port Arthur. It was lonely, those feelings welling up and nobody to talk to. I was just 'silly crazy Janis.' Man, those people hurt me. It makes me happy to know I'm making it and they're back there, plumbers just like they were."

Hearing Huddie Ledbetter ("Leadbelly") records started her singing; a trip to Los Angeles' Venice showed her she wasn't the only beatnik in the world, and at the University of Texas in Austin she fell in with the folk-music beats who lived in a rundown apartment house dubbed the Ghetto.

"She was a wild girl," recalls Travis Rivers, a Texas friend who is now manager of an excellent rock group, Mother Earth. "One time a bunch of us went to some clip joint over in Louisiana, college kids with all the toughs. Janis started dancing with some of the toughs, they started pawing her, and she bashed one of 'em on the head with a bottle. Man, did that start a fight! We were lucky to get out with our lives."

Janis sang folk music of all kinds in those days, but got her local reputation as a blues singer. ("Even then, if you heard her once, you never forgot her," said another Texas friend.) She wrote a few songs, including "Turtle Blues." But while she's written a few more since, songwriting has never become a major concern. College didn't either; after a few terms she dropped out and for five years she drifted in the folk-beat world in Texas, New York, and finally San Francisco, singing when she could, getting odd jobs or unemployment when she couldn't.

By 1965, after two years in San Francisco, it had strung her out; the years of hitchhiking, going hungry, too much drugs, and finally a dead-end romance had created a crushing burden. She ran back to Texas for a final try at being the teacher her parents wanted. For a year she lived at home, dressed like a good Texas girl, and studied hard at the Lamar State College of Technology at Beaumont. Her family was happy, her grades were good, but Janis was restless and edgy with the strain of being proper.

For San Francisco, however scary, was by then her home. North Beach and the emergent hippie community in the Haight-Ashbury were filled with people like her, wild kids (many of them, musicians particularly, from Texas) who had broken out of small towns. Like a new kind of frontiersmen, looking for psychic space and adventure, they moved west to a city traditionally the last haven for American outcasts, bringing with them a good-humored vitality, a backwoods taste for the bizarre, and an uncouth and ribald sophistication.

Those kids in 1965-66 were discovering rock 'n' roll, learning happily that, with a few freaky injections, rock could be the perfect expression-celebration of their community life style. One mover in the trend was Chet Helms, a displaced Texan who

95

as head of the Family Dog put on San Francisco's first hippie-rock dances and ran the "psychedelic" Avalon ballroom. Helms also encouraged the founding of a band called Big Brother and the Holding Company which became the Avalon's unofficial house band.

Helms was an old friend and hitchhiking pal of Janis's from their Austin days; when Travis Rivers, also a friend of Helms', got to San Francisco and heard Big Brother, he knew that Janis would be perfect for them, and that this new rock would be perfect for her. He convinced Helms and in the spring of 1966 went back to Texas, told Janis about the music and the new scene, and without one look back, she quit Lamar State College, left her family, and drove with Rivers back to the Haight.

Plunged without introduction into the crazily vibrant world of music, posters, and LSD, she sang her first dance in June, 1966. "All the Avalon regulars used to stand at the back not listening to the music and playing it cool," remembers one who was there, "but Janis sang one note, and they dropped their drinks and flocked to the front."

"It was the most thrilling time in my life," Janis recalls. "I mean, I had never *seen* a hippie dance before, man, and then I was up there in the middle of one. I couldn't believe it, all that rhythm and power. I got stoned just feeling it, like it was the best dope in the world. It was so sensual, so vibrant, loud, *crazy!* I couldn't stay still; I had never danced when I sang, just the old sit-and-pluck blues thing, but there I was moving and jumping. I couldn't hear myself, so I sang louder and louder, by the end I was wild."

The wildness was contagious. With her, Big Brother, until then fairly low in the city's rock pecking order, moved into the big three with the Jefferson Airplane and the Grateful Dead. The word of "the band with the incredible chick singer"—white girl singers were then a very rare commodity in rock—spread quickly. When Janis moaned the last notes of Big Mama Willie Mae Thornton's "Ball and Chain" at the Monterey Pop Festival in June, 1967, the stunned audience suddenly went beserk, and Janis, insane with joy, sweat dripping through the open lace of her clinging gold knit pant suit, was big time.

"She's a very sweet little girl. I think of her as my
sister, and I love her. Everybody who's ever known Janis loves
her. They have to, and she needs it. Her problem is that she knows
she's good, but she can't really believe it, so she's reaching out
all the time. A very human thing to do." (Powell St. John, Austin
friend formerly with Mother Earth.)

"I can't talk about my singing, I'm inside of it. How
can you describe something you're inside of. I can't know what
I'm doing; if I knew it, I'd have lost it. When I sing, I feel, oh,
I feel, well, like when you're first in love. It's more than sex, I

know that. It's that point two people can get to they call love, like when you really touch someone for the first time, but it's gigantic, multiplied by the whole audience. I feel chills, weird feelings slipping all over my body, it's a supreme emotional and physical experience."

She paused briefly. "I read a story about some old opera singer once, and when a guy asked her to marry him, she took him backstage after she had sung a real triumph, with all the people calling for her, made him see what it was like, then asked, 'Do you think you could give me that?' That story hit me right, man. I *know* no guy ever made me feel as good as an audience. I'm really far into this now, really committed. Like, I don't think I'd go off the road for love now, for life with a guy no matter how good. Yeah, it's the truth. Scary thing to say though, isn't it?"

She shuddered at the unpleasant thought, then, looking down at her feet, gave a squeal of delight.

"You dig my gold shoes?"—lifting one high—"I love 'em. I love wearing gold shoes, it's like a breakthrough. It demands a whole kind of attitude for a chick to wear gold shoes. I went down to I. Magnin's one day, man, and was sitting in the shoe place with all these chic, modely girls and all these chic, modely shoes, and I bought *two* pairs of gold sandals. It was a very strong thing, a very affirmative trip. Maybe only girls would understand, but it felt almost as good as singing."

She was in her apartment, a cramped four-roomer high on a hill in the Mission District. She and her roommate Linda, a strikingly handsome dark-haired girl who prefers to be last-name-less, have decorated it with a loving carelessness, covering walls with posters and photographs and cartoons, the floor with Oriental rugs, and every available space with Victoriana and assorted bric-a-brac, including Charley (the Siamese fighting fish in a wine bottle), Gabriel (the waist high statue of a penis), and George (Janis's dog and best friend). Fittingly, most care has been lavished on Janis's bedroom which, swathed in Indian canopies, scented by incense, and lit by bulbs with purple flowers as filaments, has a romantic bordello ambience.

Working with the new band has meant two solid months in San Francisco and Janis likes that. She gets to make her own brown rice and salads—she's proudly dieted off 15 pounds—shops, tools around in her Porsche that a friend painted

98

like a flowing mural of the universe with rainbows, astrological signs, a bloody American flag, and Big Brother included; she sees old friends, gets free drinks at the Coffee Gallery on Grant Avenue (a hangout since her North Beach days), and parties until she can't stand up anymore. Linda makes her more new clothes, and her gentle seriousness has a calming, restful effect on Janis.

The last time she really lived in San Francisco was over a year ago. She lived in the Haight, had a listed phone number, and was only becoming a star. Now the city, her apartment, and friends are like a retreat, her only real world.

"The whole success thing has been weird," she said. "I had never said, 'I am a singer.' I was just Janis; singing was something groovy I could do without compromising myself. But now I look around after the violent changes I've been through in the last year, and I see how surreal it's gotten.

"See the Playboy poll? Best Chick Singers: Aretha [Franklin], Dionne Warwick, then me. Too much! Flying around in airplanes, kids screaming, a lot of money and people buying me drinks. I can understand $100, but not $10,000. Money was always what I had in my pocket. What's that stuff in the banks?

"There's a fantasy at work that can suddenly click in. Like I went to this neighborhood fish store, and the girl at the counter said, 'Aren't you somebody, that singer, that . . .' and then she got red and started babbling about how she went to Las Vegas and L.A. and she never saw *anybody* and now right in her store, etc.—and it was me she was talking about! Or like making it at the Newport Folk Festival. Back in Texas I was always looking for somebody to hitch with me to it, and last year, the first time I go, *Janis* is the star. I dug it, man.

"That fur coat, too. Know how I got that? 'Southern Comfort!' Far out! I had the chick in my manager's office photostat every goddam clipping that ever had me mentioning 'Southern Comfort,' and I sent them to the company, and they sent me a whole lotta money. How could anybody in their right mind want *me* for their image? Oh, man, that was the best hustle I ever pulled—can you imagine getting paid for passing out for two years?"

By this time she was laughing so hard that she was jumping up and down, but in a minute she had subsided enough

David Gahr

to start rapping again—Janis in full swing is one of the great, all-time word-tumbling-on-word rappers.

" 'Course there's reality, too. Fantasy and reality, that's how I see things. That's why I called my company—a company, dig that, man—Fantality, to get both in. Reality is cold dressing rooms, lousy food, sitting alone in motel rooms having to watch TV, stewardesses and people on airplanes treating you like a freak, lousy halls and bad sound, playing for people you don't feel you can relate to, people out there in Kokomo who just look *at* you, at your outsides, like *curious*. Guys on the road at least have girls they can pick up, but who are the boys who come to see me— thirteen years old, man."

Go on the road, she said, and the only thing that can keep you going is the music. The rap slowed down; she had to explain why she left Big Brother and that was hard.

Long before it happened, the breakup had been no secret and, in fact, had been considered inevitable. From Monterey onward Janis was increasingly singled out until promoters were advertising "Janis Joplin with Big Brother and the Holding Company." Reviewers lauded Janis consistently and put down the band almost as consistently. The band, many said, was not good enough for her and she was wasting energy pulling them along. On record, without the electricity of live performance, the group sounded amateurish. But the band, which had more drive and originality than they were given credit for, didn't want to be her backing group. Janis, insecure about her own position and ambitions, thought they were trying to make her feel guilty for having more talent. Fights, at first discreet, broke out in dressing rooms and then on stage; the very fact of uncontrollable fighting, which seemed a failure of the whole hip spirit, added to the bitterness.

"It was a very sad thing, man," Janis said. "I love those guys more than anybody else in the whole world; they know that. But if I had any serious idea of myself as a musician, I had to leave. Getting off, real *feeling*, like Otis Redding had, like Tina Turner, that's the whole thing of music for me.

"But by the end we were shucking. We worked four, six nights a week for two years, man, doing the same tunes, and we'd put everything into them we could. I was jumping and dancing and all, but I was lying, and I'd go off stage and feel like

102

the world's biggest bullshitter. I don't mind selling pleasure if people want to pay for it, but who wants to get paid ten grand for *acting* like you're having a good time? That's shameful, and I saw it before the band saw it. That's what happened."

"The shucking thing, that's her judgment," says Peter Albin, Big Brother's bass player, but otherwise, he sees much the same picture: the claustrophobic effects of long tours with no rehearsal time, delivering the formula songs the audience demanded. "Janis was the best musician; she could experiment on stage; we needed time and rest to do new things. So for us it got to the point where all we wanted to do was play our tunes and split the stage."

"It was a hard time," Albin says. "For a while there, for us all even being in the same room was a total stone drag. But after we knew it was over, it started to get good again, and now all of us are working hard and moving."

> *Call me mean, call me evil, I've been called*
>   *much worse things around,*
> *Call me mean, call me evil, I've been called*
>   *much worse things around,*
> *But I'm gonna take good care of Janis, honey,*
>   *yeah, ain't no one gonna dog me down.*
>   —"Turtle Blues"

It was another evening back at rehearsal and worries. The whole process of assembling a new band had been frustrating; Janis had help—her manager, Albert Grossman, the sharp-eyed grandfather of new rock management, collected and auditioned some of the musicians, and Nick Gravenites and guitarist Mike Bloomfield suggested arrangements and worked the band into shape—but the pressure was on her.

A few days before their first date (not counting the disappointing preview at the Stax-Volt Christmas Show in Memphis) they didn't even have a name. Janis and Charley, Janis Joplin Blues Church, Janis Joplin's Pleasure Principle, even Janis Joplin and the Sordid Flavors—nothing was quite right.

But that was minor. First the organ player got drafted. Another was found and then the trumpet player left. The new musicians had to learn everything from scratch while the others tried to think of new ideas, what riffs to use, where to put vocal back-ups, how to get drama into each song, how to vary beginnings and endings. New material had to be found; old material, like "Ball and Chain," had to be reworked to set it off from Big Brother's versions.

And Janis was trying to work on her voice, but she was recovering from her twenty-sixth birthday party ("Me and Linda and two guys for two days, man, best party I ever had"). "I've been as much a folk hero as a singer so far," she said as the musicians were tuning up. "I wanna sing now. I'm exciting, but I'm not too subtle yet. Those people who say I'm like Billie Holiday. Man, I'm nowhere near her; hear her once and you know that. But my voice is getting better. People like to say I'm ruining it. Maybe it's getting rougher, but I still can reach all the notes I ever could. I don't know how long it will last. As long as I do, probably."

"Hey, Janis, what should we start with?" asked drummer Roy Markowitz.

"Nick's tune, okay?" There was general assent. The room was so cold they could see their breath.

Markowitz called the beat, the organist started with some quick chords, the bass came in, then the drums, the sax and trumpet.

"As good as you've been to the whole wide world, baby, as good . . ."* Janis sang, her heels doing little hops, her mouth almost biting the mike. Then she cut it off. Something was wrong, she said, and the others agreed, and they all suggested changes— an added chorus here, a tighter bass line, the drums a little flashier to start the ending crescendo.

They started again. Two more false starts, and then it was right, the beginning slow, then getting intense; the middle softer but still holding the new level of intensity until it broke away into the finale.

"That's how good I'm gonna be to you," Janis shouted, working as hard as she ever worked on stage for the empty attic. The music was like a river, cushioning her, carrying her, pushing her on. George, the dog, got up from his sleep and started to

---

*"AS GOOD AS YOU'VE BEEN TO THIS WORLD" by Nick Gravenites. Copyright © 1968 by Fourth Floor Music, Inc., 75 East 55th Street, New York, N. Y. 10022.

moan and uncannily he seemed to blend in.

"*As good as you've been, as good as you've been, as good as you've been*"—bam, bam, bam from the trumpet and sax —"*oh, baby, I'm gonna be just that good, oh so good to you!*" Bam-bam-bam-ba-ba-ba-aaaAPP! went the band and the song was over.

Janis Joplin, July, 1970, New York City David Gahr

On the steps of 710 Ashbury. Standing, left to right: Bill Kreutzman, Jerry Garcia, Pigpen, Bob Weir. Seated, left to right: managers Rock Scully and Danny Rifkin, and Phil Lesh

Baron Wolman

THE
GRATEFUL DEAD

But I reckon I got to light out for the Territory ahead of the rest, because Aunt Sally she's going to adopt me and sivilize me and I can't stand it. I been there before.

—Mark Twain, Huckleberry Finn

The Dead didn't get it going Wednesday night at Winterland, and that was too bad. The gig was a bail fund benefit for the People's Park in Berkeley, and the giant ice-skating cavern was packed with heads. The whole park hassle—the benefit was for the 450 busted a few days before—had been a Berkeley political trip all the way down, but the issue was a goodtimey park, so the crowd, though older and more radical than most San Francisco rock crowds, was a fine one in a good dancing mood, watery mouths waiting for the groove to come. The Airplane were on the bill too, so were Santana, the Act of Cups, Aum, and a few others; a San Francisco all-star night, the bands making home-grown music for home-grown folks gathered for a home-grown cause.

But the Dead stumbled that night. They led off with a warm-up tune that they did neatly enough, and the crowd, swarmed in luminescent darkness, sent up "good old Grateful Dead, we're so glad you're here," vibrations. The band didn't catch them. Maybe they were a bit tired of being taken for granted as surefire deliverers of good vibes—drained by constant expectations. Or they might have been cynical—a benefit for those Berkeley dudes who finally learned what a park is but are still hung up on confrontation and cops and bricks and spokesmen giving TV interviews and all that bullshit. The Dead were glad to do it, but it was one more benefit to bail out the politicos.

Maybe they were too stoned on one of the Bear's custom-brewed elixirs, or the long meeting that afternoon, with the usual fights about salaries and debt priorities and travel plans for the upcoming tour that they'd be making without a road manager, and all the work of being in the end, a rock 'n' roll band, may have left them pissed off. After abortive stabs at "Doing That Rag" and "St. Stephen," they fell into "Lovelight" as a last resort, putting Pigpen out in front to lay on his special brand of oily rag pig-ism while they funked around behind. It usually works, but not that night. Mickey Hart and Bill Kreutzman, the drummers, couldn't find anything to settle on, and the others kept trying ways out of the mess, only to create new tangles of bumpy rhythms and dislocated melodies. For the briefest of seconds a nice phrase would pop out, and the crowd would cheer, thinking maybe this was it, but before the cheer died, the moment had also perished. After about twenty minutes they decided to call it quits, ended with a long building crescendo, topping that with a belching cannon blast (which fell right on the beat, the only luck they found that night), and split the stage.

"But, y'know, I dug it, man," said Jerry Garcia the next night. "I can get behind falling to pieces before an audience sometimes. We're not *performers;* we are who we are for those moments we're before the public, and that's not always at the peak." He was backstage at the Robertson Gymnasium at the University of California at Santa Barbara, backstage being a curtained-off quarter of the gym, the other three quarters being stage and crowd. His red solid body Gibson with its "Red, White, and Blue Power" sticker was in place across his belly and he caressed-played it without stopping. Rock the manager was scrunched in a corner dispensing Tequila complete with salt and lemon to the band and all comers, particularly bassist Phil Lesh who left his Eurasian groupie alone and forlorn every time he dashed back to the bottle.

"Sure, I'll fuck up for an audience," said Mickey from behind his sardonic beard, bowing. "My pleasure, we'll take you as low and mean as you want to go."

"See, it's like good and evil," Jerry went on, his yellow glasses glinting above his eager smile. "They exist together in their little game, each with its special place and special humors. I dig 'em both. What is life but being conscious? And good and evil are manifestations of consciousness. If you reject one, you're not getting the whole thing that's there to be had. So I had a good time last night. Getting in trouble can be a trip too."

110

His good humor was enormous, even though it had been a bitch of a day. The travel agent had given them the wrong flight time and, being the day before the Memorial Day weekend, there was no space on any other flight for all fourteen of them. So they had hustled over to National Rent a Car, gotten two matched Pontiacs and driven the three hundred and fifty miles down the coast. Phil drove one, and since he didn't have his license and had six stoned backseat drivers for company, he had gotten pretty paranoid. The promoter, a slick Hollywood type, had told them at five in the afternoon that he wouldn't let them set up their own PA. "If it's good enough for Lee Michaels, it's good enough for you," he said, and they were too tired to fight it.

The Bear, who handles the sound system as well as the chemicals, was out of it anyway. When the band got to the gym, he was flat on his back, curled up among the drum cases. Phil shook him to his feet and asked if there was anything he could do, but Bear's pale eyes were as sightless as fog. By that time the MC was announcing them. With a final "Fuck it, man," they trouped up to the stage through the massed groupies.

Robertson Gym stank like every gym in history. The light show, the big-name band, and the hippie ambience faded before that smell, unchanged since the days when the student council hung a few million paper snowflakes from the ceiling and tried to pass it off as Winter Wonderland. Now it was Psychedelic Wonderland, but the potent spirits of long departed sweatsocks still owned the place. That was okay, another rock 'n' roll dance in the old school gym. They brought out "Lovelight" again; this time the groove was there, and for forty minutes they laid it down, working hard and getting that bob and weave interplay of seven man improvisation that can take you right out of your head. But Jerry kept looking more and more pained, then suddenly signaled to bring it to a close. They did, abruptly, and Jerry stepped to a mike.

"Sorry, he shouted, "but we're gonna split for a while and set up our own PA so we can hear what the fuck is happening." He ripped his cord out of his amp and walked off. Rock took charge.

"The Dead will be back, folks, so everybody go outside, take off your clothes, cool down, and come back. This was just an introduction."

Backstage was a brawl. "We should give the money back if we don't do it righteous," Jerry was shouting. "Where's Bear?"

Bear wandered over, still lost in some intercerebral space.

"Listen, man, are you in this group, are you one of us?" Jerry screamed, "Are you gonna set up that PA? Their monitors suck. I can't hear a goddam thing out there. How can I play if I can't hear the drums?"

Bear mumbled something about taking two hours to set up the PA, then wandered off. Rock was explaining to the knot of curious onlookers.

"This is the *Grateful Dead,* man; we play with *twice* the intensity of anybody else; we *gotta* have our own system. The promoter screwed us, and we tried to make it, but we just can't. It's gotta be *our* way, man."

Ramrod and the other quippies were already dismantling the original PA.

"Let's just go ahead," said Pigpen. "I can fake it."

"I can't," said Jerry.

"It's your decision," said Pig.

"Yeah," said Phil. "If you and nobody else gives a good goddam."

But it was all over. Bear had disappeared, the original PA was gone, someone had turned up the houselights, and the audience was melting away. A good night, a potentially great night, had been shot by a combination of promoter burn and Dead incompetence, and at 1:00 A.M. it didn't matter who was to blame or where it had started to go wrong. It was too far gone to save that night.

"We're really sorry," Phil kept saying to the few who still lingered by the gym's back door. "We burned you of a night of music, and we'll come back and make it up."

"If we dare show our faces in this town again," said rhythm guitarist Bob Weir as they walked to the cars. The others laughed, but it wasn't really funny. They rode back to the Ocean Palms Motel in near silence.

"When we missed that plane we should have known," said Bill Kreutzman. "An ill-advised trip."

Jerry said it was more than that. They took the date because their new manager, Lenny Hart, Mickey's father, while new at the job, had accepted it from Bill Graham. The group had already decided to leave Millard, Graham's booking agency, and didn't want anymore of his jobs, but went ahead with it rather than making Hart go back on his word. "That's the lesson: take a gig to save face, and you end up with a shitty PA and a well-burned audience."

"Show biz, that's what it was tonight," Mickey Hart said softly, "and show biz is the shits."

The others nodded and the car fell silent. Road markers flicked by the car in solemn procession as the mist rolled in off the muffled ocean.

It's now five years since the Acid Tests, the first Family Dog dances, the Mime Troupe benefits, and the Trips Festival; almost the same since Donovan sang about flying Jefferson Airplane and a London discotheque called Sibylla's became the in-club because it had the first light show in Europe; three and a half since the Human Be-In, since Newsweek and then the nation discovered the Haight-Ashbury, hippies, and "the San Francisco Sound." The Monterey Pop Festival, which confirmed and culminated the insanely explosive spring of 1967, is now three years gone. The biggest rock 'n' roll event of its time, that three-day weekend marked the beginning of a new era. The Beatles (who sent their regards), the Stones, Dylan, even the Beach Boys—the giants who had opened things up from 1963 to '67—were all absent, and the stage was open for the first generation of the still continuing rock profusion. Though it was, significantly, conceived in and directed from Los Angeles, its inspiration, style, and much of its substance was San Francisco's. The quantum of energy that pushed rock 'n' roll to the level on which it resided until Woodstock came from San Francisco.

The city, once absurdly overrated, is now underrated. The process of absorption has been so smoothly quick that it is hard to remember when it was all new, when Wes Wilson posters were appearing fresh every week, when Owsley acid was not just a legend or mythical standard, when only real freaks had hair down past their shoulders, when forty-minute songs were revolutionary, and when a dance was not a concert but a stoned-out bacchanal. But it was real; had it not been so vital it would not have been

113

so quickly universalized. After 1966 rock 'n' roll came to San Francisco like the mountain to Mohammed.

Its only two rivals have been Memphis and Nashville— like San Francisco, small cities with local musicians who, relatively isolated (by choice), are creating distinctive music that expresses their own and their cities' life styles. Musicians everywhere have been drawn to both the music and ambience of the three cities, just as jazzmen were once drawn to New Orleans, St. Louis, and Kansas City. Rock 'n' roll has always been regional music on the lower levels, but success, as much for the Beatles and Dylan as for Elvis or James Brown, always meant going to the big city, to the music industry machine. That machine, whether in London, New York, or Los Angeles, dictated that the rock 'n' roll life was a remote one of stardom which, with a complex structure of fan mags and fan clubs, personal aides, publicity men, limited tours, and carefully spaced singles, controlled the stars' availability to the public for maximum titillation and maximum profit. The fan identified with his stars (idols), but across an uncrossable chasm. The machine also tended either to downplay the regional characteristics of a style or exaggerate them into a gimmick. A lucky or tough artist might keep his musical roots intact, but few were able to transfer the closeness they had with their first audience to their mass audience. To be a rock 'n' roll star, went the unwritten law, you had to go downtown.

San Francisco's major contribution to rock was the flaunting of that rule. The Beatles had really started it; on one hand the most isolated and revered group, they were also the most personal; you knew the image, of course, not the real them, but the image was lively and changing. The same is true for Dylan, but San Francisco made it real. The early days at the Fillmore and Avalon were not unlike the months that the Rolling Stones played the Crawdaddy Club in Richmond, but for the first time there was the hope that those days would never have to end. The one-to-one performer-audience relationship was what the music was about. San Francisco's secret was not the dancing, the light shows, the posters, the long sets, or the complete lack of stage act, but the idea that all of them together were the creation and recreation of a community. Everybody did their thing and all things were equal. The city had a hip community, one of bizarrely various people who all on their own had decided that they'd have to find their

Herb Greene

own way through the universe; the old ways wouldn't do no more. In that community everybody looked like a rock star, and rock stars began to look and act and live like people, not gods on the make. The way to go big time was to encourage more people to join the community or to make their own; not to enlarge oneself out of it into the machine's big time. San Francisco said that rock 'n' roll could be making your own music for your friends—folk music in a special sense.

Sort of; because it didn't really work. Dances did become concerts, groups eagerly signed with big record companies from LA to New York, did do long tours, did get promo men, secluded retreats, Top-40 singles, and did become stars. Thousands took up the trappings of community with none of its spirit; the community itself lost hope and direction, fought bitterly within itself, and scattered. San Francisco was not deserted for the machine as Liverpool had been, but the machine managed to make San Francisco an outpost of itself. Janis Joplin is still the city's one superstar, but the unity of the musical-social community has effectively been broken; musicians play for pay, audiences pay to listen. There is now a rock musician's community which is international, and it is closer to the audience community than ever before in rock's history, but the San Francisco vision has died (or at least hibernated) unfulfilled. There are many reasons: bad and/ or greedy management, the swamping effect of sudden success, desperation, lack of viable alternatives, and the combined flatteries of fame, money, and ridiculous adulation on young egos.

But the central reason is that rock is not folk music in that special sense. The machine, with all its flashy fraudulences, is not a foreign growth on rock, but its very essence. One cannot be a good rock musician and, either psychically or in fact, be an amateur, because professionalism is part of the term's definition. Rock 'n' roll, rather than some other art, became the prime expression of that community because it was rock, machine and all, the miracle beauty of American mass production, a mythic past, a global fantasy, an instantaneous communications network, and a maker of superheroes. There's no way to combine wanting that and wanting "just folks" too. The excitement of San Francisco was the attempt to synthesize these two contradictory positions. To pull it off would have been a revolution; at best San Francisco

116

made a reform. In the long haul its creators, tired of fighting the paradox, chose modified rock over folk music.

All except the Grateful Dead, who've been battling it out with that mother of a paradox for years. Sometimes they lose, sometimes they win.

True fellowship among men must be based upon a concern that is universal. It is not the private interests of the individual that create lasting fellowship among men, but rather the goals of humanity . . . If unity of this kind prevails, even difficult and dangerous tasks, such as crossing the great water, can be accomplished.

—The I Ching, *13th hexagram:*
"Fellowship with Men"

The Grateful Dead are not the original San Francisco band—the Charlatans, the Great Society, and the Airplane all predate them, even in their Warlock stage—and whether they are the best, whatever that would mean, is irrelevant. Probably they are the loudest; someone once described them as "living thunder." Certainly they are the weirdest, black satanic weird and white archangel weird. As weird as anything you can imagine, like some horror comic monster who besides being green and slimy, happens also to have seven different heads, a 190 IQ, countless decibels of liquid fire noise communication, and is coming right down to where you are to gobble you up. But if you can dig the monster, bammo, he's a giant puppy to play with. Grateful Dead weird, ultimately, and what an image that name is. John Lennon joked about the flaming hand that made them Beatles, but Jerry Garcia is serious:

"Back in the late days of the Acid Tests, we were looking for a name. We'd abandoned the Warlocks; it didn't fit anymore. One day we were all over at Phil's house smoking DMT. He had a big Oxford dictionary, I opened it, and there was 'grateful dead,' those words juxtaposed. It was one of those moments, y'know, like everything else on the page went blank, diffuse, just sorta *oozed* away, and there was GRATEFUL DEAD, *big* black letters *edged* all around in gold, man, blasting out at me, such a stunning combination. So I said, 'How about Grateful Dead?' and that was it."

The image still resonates for the Dead; they are, or desire to become, the grateful dead. Grateful Dead may mean whatever you like it to mean, life-in-death, ego death, reincarnation, the joy of the mystic vision. Maybe it is Rick Griffin's grinning skull balancing on the axis of an organic universe that is the cover of *Aoxomoxoa,* their third record. It doesn't matter how you read it, for the Dead, as people, musicians, and a group, are in that place where the meanings of a name or event can be as infinite as the imagination, and yet mean precisely what they are and no more.

In their first beginning they were nothing spectacular, just another rock and roll band made up of suburban ex-folkies who, in '64 and '65, with Kennedy dead, the civil rights movement split into black and white, Vietnam taking over from ban-the-bomb, and with the Beatles, Stones, and Dylan, were finding out that the sit-and-pluck number had run its course. Jerry had gone the whole route: digging rock in the mid-fifties, dropping into folk by 1959, getting deep into traditional country music as a purist scholar, reemerging as a brilliant bluegrass banjo player, and then, in 1964, starting Mother McCree's Uptown Jug Champions with Pigpen and Bob Weir, who had skipped from boarding school to boarding school before quitting entirely, and got his real education doing folk gigs and lying about his age. "I was seventeen," he says, "looked fifteen, and said I was twenty-one." Pigpen, *ne* Ron McKernan, is the son of an early white rhythm and blues DJ, and from his early teens had made the spade scene, playing harp and piano at parties, digging Lightning Hopkins, and nursing a remarkable talent for spinning out juiced blues raps. All three were misfits; Jerry had dropped out of high school too to join the army, which kicked him out after a few months as unfit for service. "How true, how true," he says now.

But the Jug Champions couldn't get any gigs, and when a Palo Alto music store owner offered to front them with equipment to start a rock band, they said yes. Bill Kreutzman, then Bill Sommers to fit his fake ID, became the drummer. A fan of R & B stylists, he was the only one with rock experience. At first the music store man's son was the bass player, but concurrently Phil Lesh, an old friend of Jerry's, was coming to a similar dead end in formal electronic music, finding less and less to say and fewer people to say it to. A child violinist, then Kenton-style jazz trumpeter and arranger, he went to a Warlock gig on impulse and the group knocked him out. "Jerry came over to where I was sitting and said 'Guess what, you're gonna be our bass player.' I had never played bass, but I learned sort of, and in July, 1965, the five of us played our first gig, some club in Fremont."

For about six months the Warlocks were a straight rock and roll band. No longer. "The only scene then was the Hollywood hype scene; booking agents in flashy suits, gigs in booze clubs, six nights a week, five sets a night, doing all the R & B-rock standards. We did it all," Jerry recalls. "Then we got a regular job at a Belmont club, and developed a whole malicious thing, playing songs longer and weirder, and louder, man. For *those* days it was loud, and for a bar it was ridiculous. People had to scream at each other to talk, and pretty soon we had driven out all the regular clientele. They'd run out clutching their ears. We isolated them, put 'em through a real number, yeah."

The only people who dug it were the heads around Ken Kesey up at his place in La Honda. All the Warlocks had taken acid ("We were already on the crazy-eyed fanatic trip," says Bob Weir), and given dozens of mutual friends, it was inevitable that the Warlocks would play at La Honda. There they began again.

"One day the idea was there: Why don't we have a big party and you guys bring your instruments and play, and us Pranksters will set up all our tape recorders and bullshit, and we'll all get stoned. That was the first Acid Test. The idea was of its essence formless. There was nothin' going *on.* We'd just go up there and make something of it. Right away we dropped completely out of the straight music scene and just played the Tests. Six months; San Francisco, Muir Beach, Trips Festival, then LA."

Jerry strained to describe what those days were like, because, just as it says in Tom Wolfe's *Electric Kool-Aid Acid Test,* the Dead got on the bus, made that irrevocable decision that the only place to go is further into the land of infinite recession that acid opened up. They were not to be psychedelic dabblers, painting pretty pictures, but true explorers. "And just how far would you like to go in?" Frank asks the three kings on the back of *John Wesley Harding.* "Not too far but just far enough so's we can say that we've been there," answer the kings. Far enough for most, but not for the Dead; they decided to try and cross the

119

great water and bring back the good news from the other side. Jerry continued,

"What the Kesey thing was depended on who *you* were when you were there. It was open, a tapestry, a mandala—it was whatever you made it. Okay, so you take LSD and suddenly you are aware of another plane, or several other planes, and the quest is to extend that limit, to go as far as you can go. In the Acid Tests that meant to do away with old forms, with old ideas, try something *new*.

"When it was moving right, you could dig that there was something that it was getting toward, something like ordered chaos, or some *region* of chaos. The Test would start off and then there would be chaos. Everybody would be high and flashing and going through insane changes during which everything would be *demolished*, man, and spilled and broken and affected, and after that, another thing would happen, maybe smoothing out the chaos, then another, and it'd go all night til morning.

"Just people being *there,* and being responsive. Like, there were microphones all over. If you were wandering around there would be a mike you could talk into. And there would be somebody somewhere else in the building at the end of some wire with a tape recorder and a mixing board and earphones listening in on the mikes and all of a sudden something would come in and he'd turn it up because it seemed appropriate at that moment.

"What you said might come out a minute later on a tape loop in some other part of the place. So there would be this odd interchange going on, electroneural connections of weird sorts. And it was people, just *people,* doing it all. Kesey would be writing messages about what he was seeing on an opaque projector and they'd be projected up on the wall, and someone would comment about it on a mike somewhere and that would be singing out of a speaker somewhere else.

"And we'd be playing, or, when we were playing we were playing. When we weren't, we'd be doing other stuff. There were no sets, sometimes we'd get up and play for ten minutes and all freak out and split. We'd just do it however it would happen. It wasn't a gig, it was the Acid Tests where anything was OK. Thousands of people, man, all helplessly stoned, all finding themselves in a roomful of other thousands of people, none of

120

whom any of them were afraid of. It was magic, far out, beautiful magic."

Since then the search for that magic has been as important for the Dead as music, or rather, music for the Dead has to capture that magic. All of them share the vision to one degree or another, but its source is essentially Jerry Garcia. "Fellowship with man" stresses the need of "a persevering and enlightened leader . . . a man with clear, convincing and inspired aims, and the strength to carry them out." Some call Jerry a guru, but that doesn't mean much; he is just one of those extraordinary human beings who looks you right in the eyes, smiles encouragement, and waits for you to become yourself. He can be vain, self-assertive, and even pompous, but he doesn't fool around with false apology. More than anything else he is cheery—mordant and ironic at times, but undauntedly optimistic. Probably really ugly as a kid—lumpy, fat-faced, and frizzy haired—he is now beautiful, his trimmed hair and beard a dense black aureole around his beaming eyes.

Phil Lesh, Jerry's more explosive and dogmatic other half, comes right out and says that the Grateful Dead "are trying to save the world," but Jerry is more cautious. "We are trying to make things groovier for everybody so more people can feel better more often, to advance the trip, to get higher, however you want to say it, but we're musicians, and there's just no way to put that idea, 'save the world,' into music; you can only *be* that idea, or at least make manifest that idea as it appears to you, and hope maybe others follow. And that idea comes to you only moment by moment, so what we're going after is no farther away than the end of our noses. We're just trying to be right behind our noses.

"My way is music. Music is me being me and trying to get higher. I've been into music so long that I'm dripping with it; it's all I ever expect to do. I can't do anything else. Music is a yoga, something you really do when you're doing it. Thinking about what it means comes after the fact and isn't very interesting. Truth is something you stumble into when you think you're going someplace else, like those moments when you're playing and the whole room becomes one being; precious moments, man. But you can't *look* for them and they can't be repeated. Being alive means to continue to change, never to be where I was before. Music is the timeless experience of constant change "

Musical idioms and styles are important to Jerry as suggestive modes and historical fact, but they are not music, and he sees no need for them to be limiting to the modern musician or listener. "You have to get past the idea that music *has* to be *one* thing. To be alive in America is to hear all kinds of music constantly—radio, records, churches, cats on the street, everywhere music, man. And with records, the whole history of music is open to everyone who wants to hear it. Maybe Chuck Berry was the first rock musician because he was one of the first blues cats to listen to records, so he wasn't locked into the blues idiom. Nobody has to fool around with musty old scores, weird notation, and scholarship bullshit; you can just go into a record store and pick a century, pick a country, pick *anything,* and dig it, make it a part of you, add it to the stuff you carry around, and see that it's all music."

The Dead, like many modern groups, live that synthesis, but the members' past experience encompasses a breadth of idiom unmatched by any other comparable band. Electronic music of all sorts, accidental music, classical music, Indian music, jazz, folk, country and western, blues, and rock itself—one or all of the Dead have worked in all those forms. In mixing them all they make Grateful Dead music, music beyond idiom, which makes it difficult for some whose criteria for musical greatness allow only individual expression developed through disciplined understanding of a single accepted idiom. A Dead song is likely to include Jerry's country and western guitar licks over Bill and Mickey's 11/4 time, with the others making more muted solo statements— the whole thing subtly orchestrated by an extended, almost symphonic, blending of themes. Whatever it is, Jerry doesn't like to call it rock 'n' roll—"a label," he says—but it is rock, free, daring music that makes the good times roll, that can, if you listen, deliver you from the days of old.

It works because the Dead are, like few bands, a group tried and true. Five have been performing together for four years; Tom, though he only joined the group full time last year because of an Air Force hitch, has been with them from the beginning. Mickey, a jazz drummer leading the straight life until two years ago, joined because Dead music was his music. After meeting Bill and jamming with him twice, he asked to join a set at the Straight Theatre. "We played 'Alligator' for two hours, man, and my mind was blown. When we finished and the crowd went wild, Jerry came over and embraced me, and I embraced him, and it's been like that ever since."

The Dead have had endless personal crises; Pigpen and Bob Weir have particularly resisted the others, Pig because he is not primarily a musician, and Bob because of an oddly stubborn pride. Yet they have always been a fellowship; "Our crises come and go in ways that seem more governed by the stars than by personalities," says Bob. Two years ago Bob and Pigpen were on the verge of leaving. Now the Dead, says Phil, "have passed the point where breaking up exists as a possible solution to any problem. The Dead, we all know, is bigger than all of us." Subsets of the seven, with names like "Bobby Ace and the Cards from the Bottom" and "Mickey Hart and the Heartbeats" have done a few gigs, and several of the Dead are inveterate jammers, but these separate experiences always loosen and enrich the larger group, and the Dead continue.

In life as well as music. When the Acid Tests stopped in the spring of 1966 and Kesey went to Mexico, the Dead got off the bus and started their own (metaphorical) bus. For three months they lived with Augustus Owsley Stanley III, the media's and legend's "Acid King," on the nothern edge of Watts in LA, as he built them a huge and complex sound system. The system was no good, say some, adding that Owsley did the group nothing but harm. Owsley was weird all right, "insistent about his trip," says Bob, keeping nothing but meat and milk to eat, forbidding all vegetables as poisons, talking like a TV set you couldn't turn off, and wired into a logic that was always bizarre and often perversely paranoid if not downright evil. But what others thought or think of Owsley has never affected the Dead; he is Owsley, and they follow their own changes with him, everything from hatred to awe to lauching at him as absurd. If you're going further, your wagon is hitched to a star; other people's opinions on the trip's validity are like flies to be brushed aside.

Their life too is without any idiom but their own: They returned to San Francisco in June, 1966, and after a few stops moved into 710 Ashbury, in the middle of the Haight. It was the first time they actually lived in the city as a group, and they became an institution. "Happy families are all alike," Tolstoy said, but the happy family at 710 was different from most, a sliding assortment of madmen who came and went in mysterious tidal patterns, staying for days or weeks or just mellow afternoons on the steps bordered with nasturtiums. A strange black wing decorated an upper window, and occasional passersby would be jolted by sonic blasts from deep in the house's entralia. Like the Psychedelic Shop, the Panhandle, the Oracle office, or 1090 Pine St. in the early Family Dog days, it was another bus, an energy center as well as a model, a Brook Farm for new transcendentalists.

124

With all the other groups in the city, they did become a band, an economic entity in an expanding market. They did well; since the demise of Big Brother, they are second only to the Airplane of the San Francisco groups and are one of the biggest draws in the business. But the Dead were always different. Their managers, Rock Scully and Danny Rifkin, were of the family, stoned ten-thumbed inefficiency. While other groups were fighting for recognition, more and bigger gigs, the Dead played mostly for free. Monterey was a godsend of exposure to most groups, but the Dead bitched about it, arguing that it should be free or, if not, the profits should go to the Diggers; refusing to sign releases for the film that became *Monterey Pop!* and finally helping to organize a free festival on a nearby campus and stealing banks of amps and speakers for an all-night jam (they were, eventually, returned).

But of course they did go; maybe Monterey was an "LA pseudo-hip fraud," but the Dead were a rock band as well as a psychedelic musical commune, and they knew it. The problem was combining the two. The spirit that had energized the early days was changing and becoming harder to sustain. The formlessness was becoming formalized; artifacts, whether posters, clothes, drugs, or even the entire lifestyle, became more important than the art of their creation.

"The Acid Tests have come down to playing in a hall and having a light show," Jerry says. "You sit down and watch and of course the lights are behind the band so you can see the band *and* the lights. It's watching television, loud, large television. That form, so rigid, started as a misapprehension anyway. Like Bill Graham, he was at the Trips Festival, and all he saw was a light show and a band. Take the two and you got a formula. It is stuck, man, hasn't blown a new mind in years. What *was* happening at the Trips Festival was not a rock 'n' roll show and lights, but that *other* thing, but if you were hustling tickets and trying to get a *production* on, to put some of the *old* order to the chaos, you couldn't feel it. It was a sensitive trip, and it's been lost."

Yet in trying to combine their own music lifestyle with the rock and roll business, they have missed living the best of either. Their dealings with the business world have been disastrous. Money slips through their fingers, bills pile up, instruments are repossessed, and salaries aren't paid. The group is sixty thousand dollars in debt and those debts have meant harm to dozens of innocent people. "I remember times we've said, 'that cat's straight, let's burn him for a bill,' " says Phil Lesh.

It is not that they can't be commercially successful. Their basic sound is hard rock/white R & B slightly freaked—not very different from Steppenwolf's, Creedence Clearwater's, or the Sir Douglas Quintet's. "Golden Road to Unlimited Devotion," their 1967 single, could quite easily be a hit single today. They would have been happy had success come to them; unsought success, a gift of self-amplification, is a logical extension of electrifying instruments. But they just won't and can't accept even the machine's most permissive limits. Their basic sound is just that, something to build from, and they know intuitively if to their own frustration, that to accept the system would to them be fatal. "Rendering to Caesar what is Caesar's is groovy," says Phil, "as long as you render to God what is God's. But now Caesar demands it all and we gotta be straight with God first."

They see themselves as keepers of the flame. Smoking grass on stage, bringing acid to concerts, purposely ignoring time limits for sets, telling audiences to screw the rules and ushers and *dance*—those are just tokens. In late 1967 they set up the Great Northwestern Tour with the Quicksilver Messenger Service and Jerry Abrams' Headlights, completely handling a series of dates in Oregon and Washington. "No middlemen, no bullshit," said Rock Scully. "We did it all, posters, tickets, promo, setting up the halls. All the things promoters say you can't do, we did, man, and 'cause we weren't dependent, we felt free and everybody did. That told us that however hard it gets, *it can be done,* you don't have to go along."

Out of that energy came the Carousel Ballroom. The Dead, helped by the Airplane, leased a huge Irish dance hall in downtown San Francisco and started a series of dances that were a throwback to the good old days. But running a good dance hall means taking care of business and keeping a straight head. The Carousel's managers did neither. They made absurdly bad deals, beginning with an outlandish rent, and succumbed to a destructive fear of Bill Graham. The spring of 1968, with the assassinations of Martin Luther King and Robert Kennedy, was hard on show business everywhere. Graham, in the smaller Fillmore smack in the center of an increasingly unfriendly ghetto, was vulnerable and ready to be cooperative. But to the Dead and their friends he was big bad Bill Graham, the villain who had destroyed the San Francisco scene. So as the Carousel sank further into debt, they refused the help he offered. Inevitably they had to close; Graham moved swiftly, took up the lease, and renamed the place the Fillmore West. The Dead were on the street again, licking their wounds, self-inflicted and otherwise.

Two years later they are still in the street; they are not quite failures by accepted business terms but certainly have been stagnated by their own stubborn yearning. A bust in the fall of 1967 and the increasing deterioration of the Haight finally drove them from 710 in 1968; similar hassles may drive the remnants of the family from their ranch in Novato. And the band members now all live in separate houses scattered over San Francisco and Marin County. They are still talking of making a music caravan, traveling from town to town in buses like a circus. They know a new form has to be found; the "psychedelic dance-concert" is washed up, but what is next? Maybe a rock 'n' roll rodeo, maybe something else that will just happen when the time comes. They don't know, but they are determined to find it. It is hard to get your thing together if your thing is paradise on earth. "We're tired of jerking off," says Jerry. "We want to start fucking again."

Seven o'clock Friday morning Santa Barbara was deep in pearly mist, and Jerry Garcia was pacing back and forth in an alley behind the motel, quietly turning on. One by one, yawning and grunting, the others appeared and clambered into the Pontiacs. It was the start of a long day: 8:00 A.M. flight to San Francisco, change planes for Portland, crash in the motel until the gig, play, then get to bed and on to Eugene the next day. There was neither time nor energy for postmortems; the thing to do was to get on with it.

At 7:30 Lenny Hart was fuming. The Bear was late again. Where was he? No one knew. Lenny, square-faced and serious, drummed on the steering wheel. "We gotta go, can't wait for him. What's so special about Bear that he can't get here like everyone else?" Phil started back to the motel to find him, but then out he came, sleepy but dapper in a black leather shirt and vest, pale blue pants, and blue suede boots. Lenny's eyes caught Bear's for an instant, then he peeled out.

No one missed the confrontation: Lenny and the Bear, like two selves of the Dead at war, with the Dead themselves sitting as judges. Lenny, a minister who has chosen the Dead as his mission, is the latest person they've trusted to get them out of the financial pit. The Bear, says Jerry, is "Satan in our midst," friend, chemist, psychedelic legend, and electronic genius; not a leader, but a moon with gravitational pull. He is the prince of inefficiency, the essence at its most perverse of what the Dead refuse to give up. They are natural enemies, but somehow they have to coexist for the Dead to survive. Their skirmishing has just begun.

The day is all like that, suddenly focused images that

fade one into another.

At the airport the Air West jet rests before the little stucco terminal. It is ten minutes after take-off time, and the passengers wait in two clumps. Clump one, the big one, is ordinary Santa Barbara human beings; clean, tanned businessmen, housewives, college girls going away for the holiday, an elderly couple or two, a few ten-year-olds in shorts. They are quiet and a bit strained. Clump two is the Dead, maniac, dirty, hairy, noisy, a bunch of drunken Visigoths in cowboy hats and greasy suede. Pigpen has just lit Bob Weir's paper on fire, and the cinders blow around their feet. Phil is at his twitchiest, his face stroboscopically switching grotesque leers. The Bear putters in his mysterious belted bags, Jerry discards cigarette butts as if the world was his ashtray, and Tom, one sock bright green, the other vile orange, gazes beatifically (he's a Grade Four Release in Scientology) over it all and puns under his breath.

Over on the left in the cargo area, a huge rented truck pulls up with the Dead's equipment, ninety pieces of extra luggage. Like clowns from a car, amp after amp after drum case is loaded onto dollies and wheeled to the jet's belly. It dawns on Clump One all at once that it is those arrogant heathens with all their outrageous gear that are making the plane late and keeping them, good American citizens, shivering out in the morning mist. It dawns on the heathens too, but they dig it, shouting to the 'quippies to tote that amp, lift that organ. Just about that time Phil, reading what's left of the paper sees a story about People's Park in Berkeley and how the police treated the demonstrators "like the Viet Cong." "But that's just what we are, man, the American National Liberation Front," he shouts, baring his teeth at Clump One.

Ticket takers talk politely of "Mr. Ramrod" and "Mr. Bear"; in San Francisco Airport a pudgy waitress, "Marla" stamped on the plastic nameplate pinned to her right breast, leaves her station starry-eyed and says she's so glad to see them because she came to work stoned on acid and it's been a freak-out until she saw them like angel horsemen galloping through her plastic hell; Tom, his mustachioed face effortlessly sincere, gives a beginning lecture on the joys of Scientology, explaining that he hopes someday to be an Operating Thetan (O.T.) and thus be able to levitate the group while they're playing—and of course they won't

129

ever have to plug in.

Pig glowers beneath his corduroy hat, grunting, "Ahhh, fork!" whenever the spirit moves, and the Bear starts a long involved rap about how the Hell's Angels really have it down, man, like this cat who can use a whip like a stiletto could slice open your nostrils, first the right, then the left, neat as you please, and everyone agrees that the Angels are righteously ugly.

They miss their San Francisco connection and have to hang around the airport for a couple of hours, but that somehow means that they ride first class, free drinks and all. With lunch polished off, Mickey Hart needs some refreshment, so he calls across the aisle to Ramrod, then holds his fingers to his nose significantly. Ramrod tosses over a small vial of cocaine and a jackknife, and Mickey, all the while carrying on an intense discussion about drumming, sniffs up like he was lighting an after dinner cigar: "Earth music is what I'm after"—sniff—"the rhythm of the earth, like I get riding a horse"—sniff, sniff—"and Bill feeds that to me, I play off of it, and he responds. When we're into it, it's like a drummer with two minds, eight arms, and one soul"—final snort, and then the vial and jackknife go the rounds. Multiple felonies in the first-class compartment, but the stewardesses are without eyes to see. The Dead, in the very grossness of their visibility, are invisible.

The plane lands in Portland. "Maybe it'll happen today," says Jerry, waiting to get off. "The first rock 'n' roll assassination. Favorite fantasy. Sometime we'll land, and when we're all on the stairs, a fleet of black cars will rush the plane like killer bettles. Machine guns will pop from the roofs and mow us down. Paranoid, huh? But, fuck, in a way I wouldn't blame 'em." No black cars though, that day anyway.

Lenny has done some figuring on the plane. "Things are looking up," he says. "We ought to have the prepaid tickets for this trip paid by the end of next week." Jerry says that's boss, and the Bear makes a point of showing off the alarm clock he got in San Francisco. Lenny takes it as a joke and says just be ready next time or he'll be left behind. Danny Rifkin brings the good news that they have a tank of nitrous oxide for the gig. Everybody goes to sleep.

The dance is at Springer's Inn, about ten miles out of town, and they start out about 9:30. A mile from the place there

130

is a huge traffic jam on the narrow country road, and they stick the cars in a ditch and walk, a few fragments in the flow to Springer's under a full yellow moon. The last time they played Portland they were at a ballroom with a sprung floor that made dancing inevitable, but Springer's is just as nice. It's a country and western place, walls all knotty pine, and beside the stage the Nashville stars of the past thirty years grin glossily from autographed photos—"Your's sincerely, Marty Robbins," "Love to Y'all, Norma Jean," "Warmest regards, Jim Reeves." "You got a bigger crowd than even Buck Owens," says the promoter and Jerry grins. It is sardine, ass-to-ass packed, and drippingly hot inside.

The band stands around the equipment truck waiting for the Bear to finish his preparations. Someone donates some Cokes and they make the rounds. "Anyone for a lube job," Bill calls to the hangers-on. "Dosed to a turn," says Phil. Jerry, already speechlessly spaced on gas, drinks deep. They are all ready.

It seems preordained to be a great night. But preordination is not fate; it comes to the elect, and the elect have to work to be ready for it. So the Dead start out working; elation will come later. "Morning Dew" opens the set, an old tune done slow and steady. It is the evening's foundation stone, and they carefully mortise it into place, no smiles, no frills. Phil's bass is sure and steady, Bill and Mickey play almost in unison. Then Bob sings "Me and My Uncle," a John Phillips tune with a country rocking beat. They all like the song and Bob sings it well, friendly and ingenuous. Back to the groove with "Everybody's Doing that Rag," but a little looser this time. Jerry's guitar begins to sing, and over the steady drumming of Bill, Mickey lays scattered runs, little kicks, and sudden attacks. Phil begins to thunder, then pulls back. Patience, he seems to be saying, and he's right: Jerry broke a string in his haste, so they pull back to unison and end the song. But Jerry wants it bad and is a little angry.

"I broke a string," he shouts at the crowd, "so why don't you wait a minute and talk to each other. Or maybe talk to yourself, to your various selves"—he cocks his head with a glint of malice in his eyes—"can *you* talk to your *self*? Do you even know you have selves to talk to?"

The questions, contemptuous and unanswerable, push the crowd back—who is this guy asking us riddles, what does he *want* from us anyway? But the band is into "King Bee" by that time. They hadn't played that for a while, but it works, another building block, and a good way to work Pig into the center, to seduce him into giving his all instead of just waiting around for "Lovelight." It is like the Stones but muddier—Pigpen isn't Mick Jagger after all. Jerry buzzes a while right on schedule, and the crowd eases up, thinking they were going to get some nice blues. The preceding band had been good imitation B. B. King, so maybe it would be a blues night. Wrong again.

"Play the blues!" shouts someone in a phony half-swoon.

"Fuck you, man," Mickey shouts back. "Go hear a blues band if you want that, go dig Mike Bloomfield."

Another punch in the mouth, but the moment is there, and the audience's stunned silence just makes the opening gong of "Dark Star" more ominous. In that silence music begins, steady and pulsing. Jerry, as always, takes the lead, feeling his way for melodies like paths up the mountain. Jerry, says Phil, is the heart of the Dead, its central sun; while they all connect to each other, the strongest bonds are to him. Standing there, eyes closed, chin bobbing forward, his guitar in close under his arm, he seems pure energy, a quality like but distinct from sexuality, which, while radiating itself outward unceasingly and unselfishly, is as unceasingly and unselfishly replenished by those whose strengths have been awakened by his.

He finds a way, a few high twanging notes that are in themselves a song, and then the others are there too, and suddenly the music is not notes or a tune, but what those seven people are *exactly*: the music is an aural holograph of the Grateful Dead. All their fibres, nuances, histories, desires, beings are clear. Jerry and his questing, Phil the loyal comrade, Tom drifting beside them both on a cloud, Pig staying stubbornly down to earth; Mickey working out furious complexities trying to understand how Bill is so simple, and Bob succumbing inevitably to Jerry and Phil and joining them. And that is just the beginning, because at each note, at each phrase the balances change, each testing, feeding, mocking, and finally driving each other on, further and further on.

Some balances last longer than others, moments of realization that seem to sum up many moments, and then a solid groove of 'yes, that is the way it is,' flows out, and the crowd begins to move. Each time it is Jerry who leads them out, his guitar singing and dancing joy. And his joy finds new levels and the work of exploration begins again. Jerry often talks of music as coming from a place and creating a place, a place where strife is gone, where the struggle to understand ends, and knowledge is as evident as light. That is the place they are in at Springer's. However hard it is to get there, once there, you want to cry tears of ease and never leave.

The music goes fast and slow, driving and serene, loud and soft. Mickey switches from gong to drums to claves to hand-clapping to xylophone to a tin slide whistle. Then Bob grabs that away and steps to the mike and blows the whistle as hard as he can, flicking away insanely high and screeching notes. The band digs it, and lays down a building rhythm. The crowd begins to pant, shake, and then suddenly right on the exact moment with the band, the crowd, the band, everything in the whole goddam place begins to scream. Not scream like at the Beatles, but scream like beasts, twisting their faces, trying out every possible animal yowl that lies deep in their hearts.

And Jerry, melodies flowing from him in endless arabesques, leads it away again, the crowd and himself ecstatic rats to some Pied Piper. The tune changes from "Dark Star" to "St. Stephen," the song with a beat like bouncing boulders, and out of the din comes Jerry's wavering voice. "Another man gathers what another man spills," and everyone knows that means that there's nothing to fear, brothers will help each other with their loads, and suddenly there is peace in the hall. Phil, Bob, and Bill form a trio and play a new and quiet song before Mickey's sudden roll opens it out to the group, and "St. Stephen" crashes to an end with the cannon shot and clouds of sulphurous smoke.

Out of the fire and brimstone emerges the Pig singing "Lovelight," and everyone is through the mind and down into the body. Pigpen doesn't sing; Pigpen never sings. He is just Pig being Pig doing "Lovelight," spitting out of the side of his mouth between phrases, starting the clapping, telling everybody to get their hands out of their pockets and into somebody else's pocket, and like laughter, the band comes in with rock-it-to-'em choruses. The crowd is jumping up and down in witness by this time, and one couple falls on stage, their bodies and tongues entwined in mad ritual embrace. They don't make love, but in acting it out, they perform for and with the crowd, and so everyone is acting out sexual unison with Pigpen as the master of ceremonies. The place, one body, built in music, fucks until it comes, the cannon goes off one final time, and Mickey leaps to the gong bashing it with a mallet set afire by the cannon, and it makes a trail of flame and then sparks when it hits the gong, the gong itself radiating waves of sonic energy. Bill flails at the drums, Phil keeps playing the same figure over and over, faster and faster, and Jerry and Bob build up to one note just below the tonic, hold it until, with one ultimate chord, it all comes home. The crowd erupts in cheers, as the band, sodden with sweat, stumble off the stage.

"We'll be back, folks," says Jerry. "We'll be back after a break."

Bob laughs as he hears Jerry's announcement. "It's really something when you have to lie to get off the stage."

Because it's over, gone, wiped out. They gather by the equipment van, and all but Tom, still cool and unruffled, are steaming in the chill night air. The moon has gone down, the stars are out, and there is nothing more to be done.

James Gray

THE
ROLLING STONES

There's no business like show business;
Like no business I know;
Everything about it is appealing,
Everything the traffic will allow.*

IRVING BERLIN

You can't always get what you want;
You can't always get what you want,
You can't always get what you want,
But if you try some time,
You just might find,
You get what you need.†

MICK JAGGER-KEITH RICHARD

Four A.M. on the first day of December—thirty more days until 1970—and it is bitter, bitter cold in West Palm Beach, Florida. Or, to be exact, at the Palm Beach International Raceway, a funky little redneck dragstrip a few inches above the waterline of a bush league Everglades fifteen miles (plus a few thousand social light years) from the palm fringed luxury of the coast. Thirty thousand kids are huddled before a makeshift stage vainly trying to stop the insistent wind from pushing the swamp's primeval damp through every hole in their torn army jackets, dirty sleeping bags, raveled sweaters and patched-up jeans. A few campfires make cozy orange patches in the dark, and the stage scaffolding looms skeletonlike against the cloud-flecked sky.

They've been there, this little fragment of the Wood-stock Nation, for three days of music and misery (naturally it rained) that has become a ritual for a generation. "Everybody must get stoned," said Bobby Dylan in the pun of the decade, and these kids, radiantly happy and hopeful in a squalor as total as it is voluntary, are living it. Even in the dark the faces are familiar—teenagers still pimpled with their hair just barely long, clean cut but trying to be less so, adolescents awkwardly making the shift from beer and cars to grass and "love." There are a few hippies who have been doing it for years, but most of the kids—it is *Florida*, after all—have just begun to "do their thing." Their yearning to come together (Where does it come from?), to experience that love-in, festival feeling they've heard so much about, floods up to the stage in waves of expectation so trusting and naive as to be at once absurd and deeply moving.

It's the last night of the Palm Beach Pop Festival, the smallest, last, and least fashionable festival of the year, and it barely came to pass. Southern Florida, land of orange groves and the American Legion, had responded to a Miami festival and Door Jim Morrison's supposed self-exposure with a hysterical decency campaign manipulated by grown-ups (!) like Jackie Gleason and Art Linkletter. It wanted no more festivals. From the moment that thirty-one-year-old promoter Dave Rupp announced the PBPF, "the Establishment," as he called it, tried to stop him. He was kept in court until a week before opening day, defending himself on a dozen legal fronts. His business, Dave Rupp Auto Brokers, was burned to the ground; his wife Sheila, a kindergarten teacher, was told, "It's trash like you that's making our kids turn out the way they are"; the insurance on the drag strip in which he is a partner was canceled, politicians threatened mass drug arrests, and he and his family were ostracized by their neighbors.

But the tract-home Bermuda shorts conservatives of West Palm Beach hadn't reckoned with Dave Rupp. Soft-spoken, sandy-haired and a self-described straight, Rupp is a fifties hot-rodder who became a world champion drag racer, then Wichita, Kansas rock club owner (he assembled the Kingsmen of "Louie Louie" fame), then high performance car dealer. He never forgot what it was to be an American teenager. "The cops are pigs and the kids are great," he says looking out from a corner of the light booth. "I've known that since the days when I was thirteen and outrunning the fuzz myself. I've lost $250,000 going through with this festival, but it's been worth it because of those kids."

So, with his business gone, deep in debt, and an outcast in his own town, Dave Rupp got his show on. Despite about one hundred drug busts and a personal visit by Governor Claude Kirk who kept the National Guard on pointless alert, it was a groove. Janis Joplin, the Jefferson Airplane, Sly and the Family Stone, and many others came and knocked themselves out. And now it is 4:00 A.M. and the biggest act of all, the group that should have been there twelve hours before and for whom the crowd has waited through the dark night, the Rolling Stones, are about to come on. At least some guy said ten minutes ago that they'd be on in three minutes, and . . . yes, there they are, Mick dancing out with an outrageous Uncle Sam hat on his beautiful head, and those kids shed the sleeping bags and blankets and leap up to cheer and cheer and cheer.

But that's the end of the story, or almost the end, and most often it's best to begin at beginnings, if you can find them . . .

> *Well, it goes from St. Louis*
> *Down to Missouri*
> *Oklahoma City looks oh so pretty,*
> *You oughta see Amarillo*
> *An' Gallup, New Mexico,*
> *Flagstaff, Arizona,*
> *Don't forget Winona,*
> *Bagdad, Barstow,*
> *Then San Bernardino—*
> *Won't you get hip to this kindly tip,*
> *An' take that California trip,*
> *Get your kicks,*
> *On Route 66.**

BOBBY TROUP

In 1967 rock 'n roll, while exploding with unprecedented energy, suffered a triple loss: the Beatles, Bob Dylan and the Rolling Stones stopped touring. The biggest draws in the business, they were also the most important musical-cultural influences on the whole rock scene. Each in a class by itself, the three together were their own class. Years before, rock's only other super-superstar, Elvis, had withdrawn into films, but the near simultaneous decisions by the Big Three shocked fans who had come to expect live contact with their idols. Their retreat created a vacuum that no one since has been able to fill.

At the time it was hard to conceive of a nontouring band—stories on the Beatles assumed they were breaking up—but now the reasons seem obvious. Rock 'n' roll touring is exhausting work; for stars who have to be guarded like the atomic bomb, it is claustrophobic and monotonous. Before 1967, almost no one listened at the concerts anyway, and for young men excited by the adult possibilities of their music, the public adulation attending it seemed a childish drag which only increased bank accounts already immeasurable. With an independence not dreamed of by earlier entertainers who feared "losing popularity," they simply stopped doing what they no longer enjoyed. None did lose popularity; all established with every record their continuing preeminence.

The rock world from which they had withdrawn changed just as they did—expanding many times over and becoming a sophisticated community that saw itself as the aesthetic and social center of its time. In live performance rock is now the greatest audience-gatherer in show business history. Provincial music when Elvis began to shake it on out in Memphis, it became a worldwide fad with the Beatles, and then, after San Francisco, an energy locus for a movement that looks like a new Children's Crusade.

None of the Big Three played at the Monterey Pop Festival, the event that signaled the opening of the new era, but they were missed. In 1967 it was still leader and follower. Woodstock, in fact Bethel, was a misdirected pilgrimage to Bob Dylan's home, but at that remarkable convention few missed the Stars because finally the *audience* was the star—any stoned kid blowing his heart out on a bamboo flute could think he was as beautiful as Paul McCartney. The Beatles had said years before that anybody could be a Beatle. On that August weekend half a million people glimpsed the grail.

Fascinating news to the Stars; they had quit touring to rest from a world that suffocated them with its wants. Now that world was as far out as the Stars themselves—maybe farther out. In 1966 the Beatles—all long-haired dropouts—were playing to hysterical and short-haired school kids. In a 1969 audience, half the kids might look as thoroughly strange as John Lennon.

And touring itself looked like it might be fun again. After a few years of settling inevitably into marriage and babies and quiet evenings, what a gas to taste again those touring pleasures, the late-night motel living, the hopped-up edge of extreme fatigue, the girls and the parties, the cities and airports flashing by. On the road again! And best of all, the thrill of playing on stage and getting the rush of moving so many thousand people to the whim of your lyric imagination. Money too, of course. The fantastic success of Cream, Jimi Hendrix, Led Zeppelin, and even such obvious frauds as Johnny Winter and Blind Faith in the spanking new civic auditoriums that dot America seemed profoundly encouraging to the money men who have always stood close behind rock 'n' roll royalty.

So in 1969 the Big Three began to talk of going out to see the rock 'n' roll army they had helped so much to call into being. The Beatles were not able to agree on a format. Dylan, encouraged by the success of his one-time back-up band, made a few lightning appearances and planned a tour. But the Rolling Stones, whose tours had always set an exactingly debauched standard, were the first to do a tour in the old full-blown, one-nighter style.

Who else but the Stones? Since the days when, freezing in London flats, they argued about soloists on old blues records, when they were huffing and puffing their way through Little Walter tunes in raggedy pubs and at debutante parties or getting their first following at the Crawdaddy Club in Richmond, the Stones have been the very toughest essence of a rock 'n' roll band. No mean thing to be, but a precise amalgam of diverse elements: a punk craftiness and sneering narcissism, a group comradeship unspoken and total, a cynical materialism that could never be bought, and a passionate love for a music that goes back to blues and boogie-woogie through rhythm and blues and all its white modifications. There was never anything metaphysical about the Stones, nor anything frilly. As hard and homeless as their name, unvarying in a densely primitive yet sophisticated simplicity, the Stones peered blankly out from their record covers and called everybody's bluff. Performers of "(I Can't Get No) Satisfaction" —one of the few perfect rock 'n' roll songs—the Stones express a unique alienation that is the germ kernel of the rock 'n' roll

141

sensibility—a profound frustration countered by an inchoate yearning for beauty.

Last spring the group conquered its final doubts and decided to plan a tour. Rhythm guitarist Brian Jones, strange, elusive Brian, did not want to go. Almost the founder of the group, he had been drifting out of its center for years. Without rancor but also without ceremony, he was replaced. In July, with new guitarist Mick Taylor, the Stones did a free Hyde Park concert which briefly held the record—250,000 kids for one sunny afternoon. Brian had drowned alone in his swimming pool two days before, but the show went on. Mick Jagger read Shelley ("Peace, peace, he is not dead, he doth not sleep—He hath but awakened from the dream of life") and released a thousand white butterflies from the stage, but who ever expected the Stones to *mourn?* The bad mean Stones are now so bad and mean that one of them is a dead man.

The concert was a huge success, and they fixed on an American tour for the fall. Mick finished up his role in *Performance* and left for Australia to make *Ned Kelley*. Shooting ran late and then a few weeks of obstructionism by the U.S. Passport office (talk about your undesirable aliens!) delayed progress again. By late October a brand new corporation called Stones Promotions Ltd. had a tour itinerary—nineteen concerts in fourteen cities— that would start on the Coast and work its way East. The Stones gathered in Los Angeles to finish the new record, rehearse, and soak up American vibrations from the vantage point of three mansions high in the Hollywood Hills.

Across the country the fans rushed for tickets, the most expensive for any rock concert series. Three years of incredible history, good times and bad, drugs and street fighting and growing up, and now the Stones, whose music has followed it all at a distance, were coming back to kiss off the decade. The Stones tour— say the words and you heard the sizzle of *mysto* excitement, and put your tickets in the safest corner of your drawer. What would it be like to see the Stones again? One morning I hitchhiked down from the country to San Francisco, flew to Los Angeles, and joined the tour. I had, I told my friends before I left, no idea what it would be like.

142

Take me to the station
And put me on a train
I've got no expectations
*To pass this way again.**

MICK JAGGER-KEITH RICHARD

Rolling Stones HQ (plus home for Charley Watts, his wife Shirley, baby Serafina, and assorted tour personnel) is a DuPont family house above Sunset Strip with a panoramic view of the city, a swimming pool, tennis court, and a gas fireplace in the living room that burns constantly with a steady hiss of expensive waste. Despite an impersonal rent-a-palace feeling, the Big House (as it's called) is homey. Serafina Watts toddles about the kitchen with her nanny, the cook, and the maid, watching everything with her wide grey eyes. Charley talks chess with Sam Cutler, the Stones' closest aide-de-camp ("Why does the game end when you get the king?" asks Charley. "Couldn't the pawns revolt and continue the fight on their own?"), while Ronnie Schneider, head of Stones Promotions, makes deals on the dining room phone.

The house has a cast of characters, one that with additions and deletions will remain constant for the month-long living drama. The Watts family will soon leave for England, but Charley the ever phlegmatic drummer will stay, and so will Sam, a madman Cockney passionately devoted to the well-being of "The Boys," i.e., the Stones. Ronnie too, a small, dark, and dapper businessman of twenty-six who is never without his sleekly rounded briefcase or his astonishingly vulgar humor; and Jo Bergman, Mick's personal secretary, whose democratic good temper and apparently inexhaustible patience make her an oasis of resigned sanity in times of strees.

The cast has infinite gradations, but there are essentially two groups: Stones and non-Stones. Non-Stones serve Stones, and all, down to temporary secretaries and groupie-chauffeurs, have specific functions. While record engineer Glyn Johns must be picked up at Burbank by Mary the Driver, Doreen the PR Lady must pilot Mick through days of interviews. Jo deals with the calls for free tickets while Ronnie battles with Bill Graham about the Oakland concerts and Cathy snags a car to take Shirley and Charley out shopping.

Dour Bill Belmont ("My job is logistics and keeping the goddam expenses down") is in and out, planning the movements of the sixteen-man stage crew that will be hustling fifteen tons of sound and light equipment from hall to truck to plane to truck to hall. "The best crew in the world, run of course by Chip Monck, the best stage manager in the world," he says late one night, slouching on one of the living room's three gigantic beige sofas. "Chip, after consulting with Mick, plans a theatrical approach. No crappy light shows, but a proscenium stage backlit for a changing color ambience highlighted by six Super-Trouper spots. The sound towers will be draped in grey, and Mick will sing from the center of a white starburst on a purple carpet."

His voice singsongs on about "real-time analyzers" and "acoustic voicing equipment," while Ian Stewart (Stew), sometime piano player, road manager, and lifelong friend of the Stones, plays a deft shuffle on Charley's drum kit to a Count Basie record. Other voices drift in and out: "I'll never forget my first Stones tour," says Ronnie's wife Jane, a girl of a vacuity as charming as it is natural. "I was eighteen, from a hick town, and did I have my eyes opened! I saw *everything,* be*lieve* me. Girls and girls, boys and boys, and oh, one *crazy* Negro girl who ran around the motel screaming she was *God,* for Chrissakes." Pretty Doreen (indignant): "I hung up on *Vogue* today. They asked for fourteen tickets, *fourteen!* Would they ask for fourteen tickets if it was the Beatles or Dylan?" Charley (quietly): "It was different a few years ago. We were a pack then, when Brian was alive, a family in a way. But sometimes now I'm not sure I know the others."

Next day Mick comes by from the house he shares with Keith and Mick Taylor (it's rented from Steve Stills of Crosby, Stills, Nash and Young), and is interviewed by two young rock critics from New York. Two of the best, they feel a comradeship with Jagger that they can't express and are nervously torn between awe and skepticism. Mick, dressed in green velvet, answers them with just enough boredom to keep them tense and enough informality to keep them hoping for more.

Why the tour? "I've been on the musical stage since I was five, and I've missed it for the past few years. So I said to meself, 'Back to the boards where we belong, lads.'"

White blues? "We were never hung up about not being black. We just did imitation blues, but it was always good imitation."

Popularity? "Never thought we'd be big; thought we'd do blues for the fanatics. Then we heard the Beatles' 'Love Me Do' and figured we could do music like that and not compromise, so we did."

John Lennon and Apple Records? "The trouble with John Lennon is that he's never read Marx. If he had, he'd never have tried being a pseudo-capitalist and make such a mess of it."

Politics? "I was much more political before I started music. At the London School of Whats-Is-Name, I was big on it, big arguments and thumping on tables—like everybody in *college,* man."

He smiles the Jagger smile at the room, making deep ridges beside his famous mouth; an ironic jester who insists his words, sung or spoken, don't matter at all. The interviewers leave, happy to have been there but sure he has danced beyond their range.

> *I'm sitting here thinkin' just how sharp I am,*
> *I'm sitting here thinkin' just how sharp I am,*
> *I'm an under-assistant West Coast Promo Man,*
> *So sharp, so very, very sharp.* *
>
> MICK JAGGER-KEITH RICHARD

"No, I wouldn't say we have a publicity *strategy* for this tour," says David Horowitz, the vaguely prissy PR man from Solters and Sabinson, Inc. assigned to the Stones. "The Stones, we believe, will make their own news. We see our job as facilitating the dissemination of that news as widely as possible. It's a great story and, *we* believe, an important assignment for the firm."

He's wearing a double-breasted blue blazer, a wide pink tie under a spread Italian collar, and sideburns an inch and a half longer than the nationwide norm for thirty-five-year-old males. His office is in a brand new building on Sunset Strip; the garage is full of Buick Rivieras and the elevators full of David Horowitzes—the sideburn set in pastel shirts and cuffless pants whose lifework it is to service the entertainment center of the Western world. The

145

Strip, a broad snake of a street always shedding its skin for something more glamorous, is their home, the press release and billboard their language.

Old ladies are still on the corners selling the out-of-date Movie Star Home maps, but it is rock 'n' roll, not the movies or even television, that is the "now" industry of the street. Tawdry shacks like the Whisky or Thee Experience are the public places to see and in which to be seen. Tiny boutiques with grimy dressing rooms are the centers of a fashion industry that can make yesterday's eccentricity tomorrow's old clothes. The Strip is the natural American home of the Rolling Stones. When they are not eating, sleeping or slouching about listening to records (their major occupations), they are on it.

Never to stay, but for quick jumps out of chauffered cars into Schwabs for vitamin pills and sunglasses, into this shop for a shirt, into that one for a belt and a pair of boots, into a club for a few drinks and a set of Bo Diddley, Little Richard, Taj Mahal, Chuck Berry, or the Flying Burrito Brothers. The visits—Keith and Mick are the most serendipitous—are always informal, yet somehow regal. What they buy and where they stop is of course accidental, but the Strip does not believe it. "The Stones were here last night", "Bill bought a vest here"—awed incantations that report a blessing from the gods.

The more adventuresome do not wait for a visit, but attack the citadel directly. The Stones' house is a temporary Versailles, and through it flow the suppliants, this one with a film deal, that one with a poster deal, another trying to get a record endorsement. One young man talks vaguely of his road management experience and offers his services for the tour if they'll just pay his expenses. Cool young ladies insist that Keith invited them up, and photographers and writers swear they were promised exclusive interviews. Some, even by the Strip's exacting standards, are Important—singers, producers, promoters, and groupies—but in the Stones' house they are all nervous. The Stones are in town, and all orders of caste are suddenly overturned; it's no longer Who Do You Know, but Do You Know The Stones?

The Stones themselves are distant from most of it, protected in part by the palace guard of Jo and Sam ("Let's not bother The Boys now," Sam suggests a dozen times a day in a voice that charms as it refuses), in part by their cultivated indifference to their effect, and in part too by the terrible shyness that afflicts these determined seekers at the crucial moment. Groupies of every sort who spent weeks to get to the Stones suddenly turn abject and fade into the wallpaper when confronted with one in the flesh.

"All these people, what are they *here* for?" says Charley one day to no one in particular.

"I finally figured out why I want to go home," replies Shirley, a slender blonde with large sad eyes. "It's because I'm tired of being in a house where everyone is a job and no one talks anything but numbers. 'Twenty thousand, 65 percent, dollars, seats.' And there are too many people who talk nicely to you and then don't say good-bye when they leave. Have you noticed that Charley?"

He has, but the conversation dwindles. In the dining room Ronnie is working to a climax. He's got one overambitious sideburner in a carefully laid trap, and he's springing it. What is being said is indistinct, but there is no mistaking the glow of pleasure in Ronnie's New York accent as he presses his advantage. The sideburner feints in embarrassment, looking for a safe retreat. Ronnie counters; a note of humiliation comes from the mouse in striped pants; Ronnie decides on mercy and lets his prey scurry through the kitchen to his Riviera and back to the haven of the Strip. Ronnie strolls into the living room, snapping his briefcase shut.

"Oh, these pathetic bastards," he crows. "I'll screw 'em, screw 'em all. Remember when Bill Graham came down, full of bluster, telling us he'd do the whole tour, as a favor? Listen to this, Charley, you'll get a kick out of it. There's Graham, telling me what a big shot he is, how he built the Fillmore, how he's booked this group, that group. So I sit and wait for him to finish, and then I say, 'Well, Bill, that sounds pretty good, but what did you ever do *big*?' He almost fell on the floor."

A phone rings. It's for Ronnie, and he's back at work.

At long last the tour begins, an out-of-town preview, though no one calls it that, at the University of Colorado in Fort Collins. The Stones and their entourage gather in the President's Club Room, the VIP lounge of Continental Airways at the Los Angeles Airport. A motley crew, to say the least, but the President's Club Room has seen their like—Donovan's name is scrawled a few pages back in the guest register. A few business-men are in a corner (they call it "the ghetto"), pushed there by the strange vibrations of these millionaire hippies with twelve guitar cases and their feet up on the fake Japanese furniture. One, a Bloody Mary clenched in a well-tanned hand, wanders over and notices Astrid, Bill Wyman's quiet wife.

"Well, lookee here," he calls to chuckling friend. "I think I'll sit down next to this pretty young girl, and what's your name, young lady?"

Astrid looks at Bill; Bill smiles.

"You the fellas who had the hockey game canceled for your concert?" says the friend. He's drinking Scotch. Bill says the game wasn't canceled, only moved to the afternoon.

"Aw, don't mind us," says the first. "We're from the Manned Space Center in Houston, drinking up a little rest and relaxation in California." He toasts them.

"You mean you guys are putting people on the moon?" asks Keith.

That's right," says the friend, "if Nixon will give us the money. You want to go to the moon?"

"Sure," says Keith.

"Just lemme know when," says the first.

In another corner a woman with pearls and a Chanel copy suit is showing her husband Irving pictures of their furniture in *Better Homes and Gardens*. She looks up, catching the eye of Cathy, Mick's friend and chauffeur.

"Now can you tell me which one of these boys is the father of two children by two different girls? I read about it in Cosmopolitan."

Before she can answer, Keith strides over. He has on huge purple sunglasses that obscure the top half of his face, a floor-length leather coat over his shoulders, a dirty Irish sweater, maroon velvet pants, and lizard-skin boots. A cougar tooth ear-ring is in his left ear, and his hair is a home-cut thatch that drib-bles to his shoulders.

"Are you talking about me babies?" he demands in a piercing high camp.

"I read in *Cosmo* ..."

148

"You read too many magazines, sweetie." He turns, and the lady, who must spend a lot of time with interior decorators and hairdressers, stage whispers knowingly, "I'm sure *he's* nobody's father." Keith whirls.

"Try me some time, baby."

Irving is still deep in the LA *Times*. "Irving," she whines, "Irving, they're so goddam hostile. Why, Irving, why are they?"

> *An' all the flat-top cats*
> *An' all the dungaree dolls*
> *Are headed for the gym*
> *To the sock-hop ball*
> *The joint is really jumpin'*
> *The cats are goin' wild*
> *The music really flips me*
> *Dig my crazy style!*
>
> *I'm ready,*
> *Ready, ready, Teddy,*
> *I'm ready, woooooh*
> *Ready, ready, Teddy,*
> *I'm ready,*
> *Ready, ready, Teddy,*
> *I'm ready, ready, ready, to—*
> *Rock 'n' Roll!**

(sung by) LITTLE RICHARD PENNIMAN

It's 66 degrees and sunny in Denver. The fleet of rented limousines whirs swiftly across the fall-orange prairie of the Big Sky country as the sun sinks behind the Rockies. The campus looks more like an airport or an electronics factory than a college; four hours before concert time, the kids are lining up at the doors. The Stones get there early for a sound rehearsal, and with a bored professionalism, do their jobs, calling out for more gain on the stage monitors, less treble for Bill's bass, and another mike for Charley's tom-tom.

"I don't know what it is, Chip," Mick says through his mike, "but we were *loud* in rehearsals, and now it just isn't loud."

*"READY TEDDY," words and music by John Marascalco and Robert Blackwell. Copyright © 1965 by Venice Music, Inc. and Elvis Presley Music, Inc. Used by permission.

149

Chip mumbles assent and goes back to his dials. Mick jumps down from the stage and walks to the back of the hall to listen. Coming back, he begins a little dance, a quiet hop march on the band's offbeat. His long muscular arms swing with a peculiar grace and his head is held at an angle both restful and proud. There are thirty people there, stagehands, ushers, a few girls, and they all stop to watch Mick Jagger walk. When he notices the eyes on him, he laughs, breaks stride, and then jumps back up on stage.

By eight o'clock the gym—basketball nets folded like landing gear into the ceiling—is packed. A few freaks from Denver and Boulder, but the cross section looks like a McCarthy volunteer reunion; *nice-looking* kids, smoking dope but still in knee socks and circle pins, plaid shirts and loafers. For the first time there is that soon-to-be-familiar tensely compressed energy, directed to the bright spot that waits for the Rolling Stones.

The Stones get dressed in the Letterman's Lounge, not nervous (though Charley has his usual problem of shaky feet), but as expectant as the kids. "I wonder what these kids are like now," says Keith. "I mean, do they watch TV or are they turning on in the basement?" "Or watching *Easy Rider?*" says Mick. No one knows if they'll scream; maybe they'll even be disappointed. Mick picks out a slow blues on an acoustic guitar. Keith and Mick Taylor tune up together, leaning over a small amp. Sam rushes in; it's time to go. They make a procession down the halls, carrying their guitars close so they won't get knocked out of tune. They wait at the steps as the lights dim. Sam takes the mike.

"Okay, Fort Collins, Colorado, we made it, we're here, and so I want you to give a big Western welcome to the group you've been waiting for, the *Rolling STONES!*" Up the steps and into the light. Keith's red shirt is dotted with sparkles, his black pants have silver conchos down the side. Mike is in white, a long black scarf trailing almost to the floor. He leaps high, then bows.

"All right, Fort Collins, all *right!*" There's an edge of scorn in his voice, but Fort Collins is on its feet and yelping, and Keith hammers out the first chords of "Jumping Jack Flash."

I was born in a cross fire hurricane . . . *

Yahoo! The Stones are *here!*

I was raised with a strap across my back . . .

Don't they look fine! Bill Wyman, his Fender high over his hip, standing in his customary trance. Mick Taylor bending over his Gibson, Charley snapping at the high hat, and Mick strutting like a little red rooster.

> *But it's all right now*
> *In fact it's a gas*
> *I'm Jumping Jack Flash*
> *It's a gas, gas, gas*
> *Yeah!*

A holy moment for ten thousand kids, but it doesn't get as high again. Mick never hits a peak, and the kids are shy. An eighteen-year-old freshman from Laramie is beside me, crew-cutted and in his high-school letter jacket. He's kneeling in an aisle with his date, loving it; his girl's bright brown eyes drink in Jagger's body, but they are cautious and baffled. "Street Fighting Man" closes the show; could it be their song, now or ever?

I was like any other kid, which is why all the rest identified with
me. I was just the same as they were, except that I'd jumped
the tracks a bit more, that's all. All the stuff about my leading
them and perverting them or whatever, it's a lot of cock . . .
We just sort of went along together, didn't we?
        —Mick Jagger, quoted in Playboy

, The Los Angeles Forum ("the Fabulous Forum," say the ads) is color coded. On one side all the seats, signs and mini-togas of the ushers are a garish yellow; on the other, all is an equally garish orange. It can hold eighteen thousand at full capacity and can be adapted to suit any sport, entertainment, or convention purpose; its parking lots end only where the Inglewood racetrack's lots begin; it has no windows. Swathed at night in cosmetic lighting, dreamlike and utterly free of blemish, it seems a scale model of itself. More than the new Madison Square Garden, more even than Houston's Astrodome (obviously Texas eccentric), the Forum seems a fantasy tribute to the tons of excess wealth that burden 1960s America with a Tiberian opulence.

151

The Stones are scheduled for two concerts on a single evening at the Forum; 36,000 people, mostly teenagers, have paid an average of seven dollars a seat to see them. Scalpers are getting fifty dollars for the twelve-fifty top price seats. That is but a fraction of the money spent for this evening's pleasure. The children of Los Angeles, Pasadena, Burbank, Glendale, Riverside and the other fabled freeway towns, arrive in five-thousand dollar cars designed by Detroit for the youth market, in clothes of suede and silk and exotic plastics, in boots from Italy and vests from Persia, sunglasses from Paris and belts from Mexico, bells from India and T-shirts from London. Levis, too, but more likely beige corduroy than blue denim; leather jackets, but of tailored buckskin with beaded fringe fifteen inches long. They don't look neat, because that's not the look. They are *hippies,* after all, stoned high and low on every conceivable (and therefore available) drug, but they are *rich.* Not every one, yet as they drift in clumps to their orange and yellow seats, their easy acceptance of the divine right to overconsumption is as evident as their Southern California tans.

The show starts almost two hours late—the rush conversion from the afternoon's hockey game took longer than planned—but no one minds. It's the full tour concert as the Stones planned it—perhaps the best rock show ever. Nineteen-year-old Terry Reid, the latest in a long line of handsome English guitarists, opens it with his rock-blues trio, then B. B. King does his customarily magnificent set. Ike and Tina Turner follow, and their precision choreographed rite of sexual ecstasy knocks 'em dead.

On run the Stones, Mick in black tonight, waving a big hello to Los Angeles ("Has it really been three years, Los Angeles? It doesn't feel so long."), and smiling back as he crests the wave of adulation that swarms up from the darkness. They lay it down, moving through the rockers, dropping back into blues, then "I'm Free," Mick going to the stage corners and telling the eighteen-thousand, "I'm free, I want you to be free, we gotta be free, we can be free if we know we're free." On into the sublimely evil "Midnight Rambler," and then he stops at center stage and peers out through the spotlights.

"I wish I could see all you people," he says with honeyed wistfulness. "You can see us and we're beautiful, but there are so many of you and you're probably a bit more beautiful than we are."

Mick Jagger and Chuck Berry

Ethan A. Russell

(Is *Mick Jagger* actually ceding his spotlight place to the multitude?)

"Chip, let's have some light on the people." Instantly the Forum is bright, and the crowd, freed from darkness, looks at itself, and the Stones blast into "Little Queenie," then "Satisfaction" ("Oh, we gotta find us a little satisfaction, gotta find it, and I can't find it for you, you gotta find it for yourselves"), then "Honky Tonk Woman," and the kids are on their feet, leaving the seats and pouring into the aisles, jumping over the sideburn set in the front rows, streaking to the stage, body to body, faces laughing and incredulous, Mick dancing just above their outstretched arms.

She said her name was Terri, and she appeared out of the slowly disintegrating stage-side mob, crying, shaking, and almost vomiting with fear. Shouting ushers were clearing the hall for the second show, and she dodged around them, her eye make-up smudged blackly around her tiny nose. She said she had come with her boyfriend Jim and they had been sitting up in back but had worked their way down front and then she lost him. He had her pocketbook in his jacket with all her money and she didn't know what to do.

At 1:30 A.M. poor crying Terri was a pitiful sight. Two friends and I took her out to eat (she refused everything). She said she lived in El Monte, had run away from home and was staying with friends. She didn't know their name though, and her Jim, off the next day to Viet-Nam with the Air Force, was last nameless to her too. She was scared of going home ("they'll kill me"), and every public crash pad and free clinic in LA was either closed for the night or for good. "You're a girl of our times," said Eve. "Like a rolling stone," joked Harry.

There was nothing else we could do, so we gave her a lecture on getting along with her parents until she could make it on her own, put ten dollars in her reluctant hand, and forced her into a cab that would take her to El Monte. I hope she got there.

Bukka White, an old black bluesman from Memphis, cousin and teacher of B. B. King, is backstage at the Forum, and a young white friend takes him in to meet the Stones. Keith is sitting plucking out a tune on his National steel guitar; that's

154

Bukka's instrument too, and he listens for a minute, then turns to Mick. "Why, that boy's pickin'!" says Bukka, genuinely amazed. "He's a *star*. Hey boy," and he taps Keith's knee, "you ever cut any records? You're that good, boy."

> *You can tell the men from the boys*
> *By the size of their toys.*
> —"Prospector Slim"

Oakland is next, and as the tour day drags to a start about 1:00 P.M., there arrives a singular addition to the cast, one John Jaymes, at times accompanied by his business partner Gary M. Stark, at others by his mother. John Jaymes, who is thirty, very, very fat, and whose name has been shortened from something long and Italian, is the president of a New York firm called Young American Enterprises Corp., which in turn controls the fortunes of some nineteen other companies. John is essentially a "fad merchandiser"—"fads are my basic business material." Through his companies he creates, designs, manufactures, distributes, and sells T-shirts, bumper stickers, buttons, notepads, dolls, balloons, and toys keyed to any bit of nonsense that is currently sweeping the country. One company has a contract to merchandise Rowan and Martin Laugh-In products, another makes "graffiti stationery," another is preparing to flood the country with body-painting kits. "We're getting it so good now," says John, "that if there's a fad on Monday, we'll have a button and sticker for it in the stores by Friday."

Though he claims to have made and lost millions in it, merchandising only hints at the diversity of John's interests. A one-time narcotics agent (the grass we smoke, he says, is garbage), he once ran unsuccessfully for office in New York and promoted rock 'n' roll shows at Shea Stadium. He is now setting up a youth paper to be sent free to a carefully selected list of a few hundred thousand teenage consumers, serves on a Congressional youth committee, and also does "youth promotion" for various major corporations, including Dodge cars.

How he got on the tour is a mystery, but Dodge was his angle. With him arrives a fleet of Dodges to replace the rented cars, and for every tour city similar fleets plus trucks for the equipment are promised—and maybe a Dodge executive plane from time to time. All this comes free to Stones Promotions Ltd., as does John himself. "It's a gamble for me," he says. "It's a prestige promotion for us, plus, of course, a tie-in promotion for Dodge."

Yet John's real (or maybe apparent—such distinctions lose their meaning around John Jaymes) contributions are his chutzpah and his "contacts." John, says John, can fix a ticket anywhere, make sure nobody gets busted, find hotel rooms when none are available, make scheduled airlines wait for late equipment trucks, and bluff his way through to the man at any top. "Everything's angles and how to work 'em," he says.

He meets a test the first day out. The scene: Oakland's Edgewater Inn; time: 6:00 P.M. Everyone but the Stones, Ronnie, and Sam is safely in Oakland, and the Stones plane is due any minute. In the restaurant John has a phone glued to his ear, a drink to his hand. Word comes that a few reporters and maybe one hundred kids have gathered at the airport. John smells disaster: hadn't Mick said "no reporters"? His porcine face takes on a Churchillian belligerence, the table becomes War Operations Nerve Center. Calls flash out. The airplane must land at a new spot. Impossible? He asks for a higher-up. There is none. Then the limousines must be able to drive to the airplane steps. Impossible too. He orders more drink. David Horowitz arrives and offers hushed suggestions; John waves them away. He demands that the Stones be radioed the information that an unruly mob awaits them. No. Finally he gets permission to board the plane himself and warn them in person.

Down goes the phone; doubletime through the lobby, and a seventy m.p.h. run to the airport. No limousines. He rents a few cars. "Send the bill to me." The plane lands. John is up the steps, then down. He leads The Boys out. There is one TV crew, two kids with movie cameras, and perhaps fifty others who walk politely beside the group until they reach the cars. Of which there are not enough. We all pile in, eight to a car. Screech to the motel. Mission accomplished.

The Oakland audience knows nothing of John Jaymes and his hustles. If they did, they wouldn't believe he could be connected with "their" Rolling Stones. In Oakland that night they want reality as *they* see it; a curious place, the Bay Area. This blessedly beautiful gathering of cities on still green hills beside a tranquil bay is, for its residents, a new Paris, the intellectual and moral center of the world youth avant garde. To the Bay Area mentality, Los Angeles is plastic, London frivolous, New York impossible and dirty besides. Happy in its provinciality and passionately convinced of its superiority, it believes itself a microcosm of American problems and possibilities.

Problems and possibilities, precisely; the Bay Area, a tensely schizoid union of Berkeley and San Francisco, has never decided which is more real. Since the Free Speech Movement, militant Berkeley has angrily emphasized the problems. With the Haight-Ashbury at its golden peak, good-timey San Francisco embodied the psychedelic possibilities. While the Haight decayed and fled from itself, Berkeley took acid, created, fought for, and lost a beautiful park, and now no one knows what to do. "Berkeley" and "San Francisco" have become less geographic entities than conflicting states of mind, often existing in equal strength in the same person.

Rock 'n' roll has become the prime symbol of the paradox and a bone of incessant contention. The Militant calls it a capitalist diversion and quotes Bob Dylan to prove it; The Fan mocks the Militant's paranoia, and dances, convinced that music will dissolve entrenched and profitable inequity. Both mistrust their own feelings as much as their "enemies," and the Bay Area hasn't had a community good time in years. In a summer of rock festivals, San Francisco's effort, the Wild West Show, was destroyed before it happened by the tactless extravagance of its "hip rock" backers and the concerted spite of radicals who mistook incompetence for a plot against the people.

The incestuous battling did not cease for the Stones; if anything it got more intense (and more confused). Promoter Bill Graham and San Francisco *Chronicle* columnist Ralph J. Gleason, who usually defend rock as the poetic revolution while avoiding radical attack on rock's business ethic, publicly lashed the Stones for their reactionary arrogance and greed. "Mick Jagger may be a great performer," Graham told all listeners, "but he's an egotistical creep as a person." Jagger, wrote Gleason, had personal moral responsibility for the high ticket prices and the tour's tough contracts. The radicals, who in their hearts adore the Stones for their uncompromising toughness, did their best to forget their political doubts and scrambled for tickets with the rest of the fans. Both concerts, of course, were total sell-outs.

It's all there at concert time—a community's projected doubts and wants brought together by the magic of theater into the blue-grey cavern of the Oakland Coliseum. Gathered, they focus before the stage as an invisible but palpable question that demands resolution in the music of the Rolling Stones. The Stones fend it off, avoiding questions about money and politics at a small preconcert press conference. "I think you know we're with you on Viet-Nam and everything," Mick says. "It's just that I don't find it a thing to sing songs about. It's music for us, and supposed to be fun. We want you to get up and dance, not sit back and be worried about what you're *supposed* to do."

The first concert, plagued by broken amps and erratic mikes, barely gets off the ground, but the second is a gas. Feeding on the crowd's intensity, the band plays magnificently, Keith hurling back the invisible demands in twisted, astringent lines from his transparent guitar. "I'm Free" goes dead to the crowd that's been wearing "Free Huey," "Free the Oakland 7" and "Free the Chicago 8" buttons for years—so what if *you're* free, Mick Jagger?—but when the lights come up, the crowd breaks loose on schedule. Some just dance to the music as they once did at the Fillmore, but thousands surround the stage in a sea of upraised fists, each begging Mick's approval, each asking, Which side are you on, boy?

A few bearded kids try to climb on the stage and Mick dances back from the edge, his ironic smile suddenly gone. He sings "Satisfaction" as if possessed, his head shaking in fury, but the fists still wave in his face unsatisfied. Into "Street Fighting Man," and Mick's right hand finally makes a fist that rises slowly above his head. A new wave of fists appears, but then his left rises in a V. There are scattered boos. A kid makes it over the edge; Sam scurries over to get him off. Bill Graham, eyes blazing, grabs Sam and knocks him down. The music rockets on and the two grown men roll awkwardly under the piano. In the crescendo Mick hurls back the question that is his only answer—

> But what can a poor boy do,
> 'Cept sing in a rock 'n' roll band?
> 'Cause in sleepy London town, there's just no place for a
> Street Fighting Man!*

He grabs a hatful of rose petals and flings great handfuls of them at the mob. A few acres of kids stand open-mouthed, each on some personal brink of hope and fear, and it seems that this singing poor boy is doing just fine. It's over; the Stones run from the stage.

They are disappointed; San Francisco, they had thought, was a groovy place. "Politics like that, I don't believe the intensity," says Mick. In their dressing room, the banquet Graham had ordered for them (with special English beers and cheeses) is scattered obscenely on the floor. On one wall Graham had pinned a poster of himself giving the finger to the world at large. Now food is smeared over his face, and "This is where my head is at" is written in a balloon from his grinning mouth. They'll be back—they had already promised a free San Francisco concert at the end of the tour; but tonight they hurry to John Jaymes's waiting Dodges and fly back to mansioned comfort in pleasant, if plastic LA.

And that Mick Jagger—I wouldn't take him if the price was only $3000. . . . We guessed wrong with the Rolling Stones the last time around. It was one of our biggest financial blunders. . . . The price was a bit high but it looked like a good investment. We put in wooden horses as a barrier and put a line of policemen along with them. . . . Those kids charged and rolled over everything, police, horses, and all. We wound up with some crushed policemen.

Now the Monkees, there's an improvement. Really cooperative. They opened by telling the kids, "Sit in your seats and enjoy the show." This was really good for crowd control.

—Promoter Joe Munnick of Raleigh, North Carolina, quoted in Amusement Business, *a Billboard Publication*

> *When I'm riding 'round the world*
> *An' I'm doin' this*
> *An' I'm signin' that*
> *An' I'm tryin' to make some girl*
> *Who tells me*
> *"Baby, baby, come back,*
> *Maybe next week,*
> *'Cause you see*

159

I'm on a losing streak"—
I can't get no;
*No, no, no . . .**

MICK JAGGER-KEITH RICHARD

A strange warning, that Oakland concert—what do
these kids *want* so badly from the Stones? But the message, even
if it were decipherable, is lost in the blur of concerts that follow.
With Oakland down, the opening high moments are over. Now
the body of the tour begins. Above all else, it is bloody hard work.
The hours are ridiculous; bed is seldom reached before dawn, and
once everyone is up, showered, fed, and dressed, there is time for
nothing but getting organized and to the gig. San Diego, then
Phoenix (with a 3:00 A.M. stop for the hell of it in Las Vegas
where we wander from club to club as startled patrons ask us if
we're the cast of "Hair"), then a night off before beginning a four-
day run to Dallas, Auburn, Champaign, and Chicago to wind up
the first half of the tour.

Touring—how to remember its oddness? It is a trip in
every sense: a decision to accept the discipline of a long and intense journey which, though known in form, is mysterious in con-
tent. Normal stimuli—friends, home, and daily routine—which
we all call reality, are replaced by the repetitive actions of constant
travel. Life on tour, while infinitely more *exciting* than ordinary
life, is much less varied. It has no cause and effect, only sequence;
you cannot ask yourself, "What am I going to do today?" because
you know what you have to do even though you have no idea
what's going to happen. It is a tunnel of adventure through which
you fall in wide-eyed but disoriented passivity. The more experienced conserve their energy, but the powerful tendency is to get
stoned and stay stoned on whatever combination of pills and
powders, liquids and weeds that comes your way. To leave the
tour is almost unimaginable. Moments that could be snatched for
walks, reading, or sight-seeing are passed up. When you get to
your motel room, you turn on the TV and leave it on, never changing channels, until you leave.

Undoubtedly more bizarre in detail (do candidates sniff
cocaine through tightly rolled ten dollar bills in the first-class jet

*"(I CAN'T GET NO) SATISFACTION" by Mick Jagger & Keith Richard. Copyright ©
1965 by Abcko Music, Inc. Used by permission. All rights reserved. International Copyright
Secured.

160

compartment?), the tour is more like a presidential campaign than anything else. We leap across the vastness of America in giant bounds. To everyone on whom we descend in sloppy mass—desk clerks, Avis girls, stewardesses, porters, headwaiters, and cops— we are an event ("Guess who I saw at work today, dear?"). We move in an unwieldly splendor, waiting grumpily for John Jaymes-arranged Dodges or limousines, ignoring ranks of empty cabs.

At each city is the meeting of the faithful who have already been warmed up by the introductory acts before we arrive. The Stones come on just barely in time, deliver the prepared show, bow, then roar away through the waving hands and smiling-anxious faces of well-wishers. There is no flesh-pressing. The promoter and his family, maybe a disc jockey or two, get into the dressing room to thrill for a moment in the glow of indisputable fame, but the ordinary Stones lover is kept at a distance that would appall the post-Kennedy politician. Surrounded by security men, we sweep in and out of cities, honking our way through red lights at top speed, and driving as though pursued by assassins to elude the few carloads of fans who want only an autograph and a good snap for their Instamatics.

In political terms, the Stones are the candidate, Ronnie the campaign manager, Sam the go-for and court jester, and Jo the traveling secretary and liaison with campaign headquarters—the Stones' London office with which she is in daily contact. John Jaymes is the fixer and detail man; Tony, a big and nutty black kid, the strong man; and there is even a press corps: photographer Ethan Russell, Stones biographer Stanley Booth, and myself. In Los Angeles there were always extras in our cast; on the road there are none.

The cast becomes a group—not quite a team, but a band united by the uniqueness of the joint experience. The whole tour numbers perhaps forty people, counting equipment men and supporting acts, but they travel in their own casts, converging with us only at concert time. Chip Monck, Bill Belmont, and Stew (the advance men) we see often, but B. B. King, who appeared at half the concerts, barely met the Stones. (None of "The Boys" in the whole month took the time to introduce themselves and pay their respects.) There were light men and sound technicians who, after working for a month in absolute interdependence, did not know each other's first names.

161

The dressing room of the Los Angeles Coliseum

Ethan A. Russell

Stanley, Ethan, and I have little to do but stay reasonably alert, take our notes and pictures, and be sure we're not left behind—a demanding task in itself. Everyone else has one or many jobs to do, and while everything gets done, nothing is done well enough for anyone to relax. That is in part due to Murphy's inexorable Law, in part to the last-minute scramble in which the tour was planned, and in part because there is no chief of operations. Ronnie, John, or Bill Belmont can, for instance, set the time and means for departure from hotel to gig, and they often do, in conflicting independence. When they do agree, Sam, acting on mumbled instructions from a sleepy Keith, can insist on new arrangements that will give "The Boys" another hour's sleep.

So we arrive in Dallas to find that all room reservations have been canceled because Bill had forgotten to reconfirm them. While he chews at the scarred stubs of nails long since bitten away, a furious Ronnie has a tearful desk clerk begging space from every hotel in town. The plane chartered for the Dallas to Auburn leg flies away empty on instructions from an unknown culprit. Two hours of frantic calls result in the following travel spaghetti: press corps, Jo, Stew, and Terry Reid fly Delta to Atlanta and rent cars for a three-hour drive to Auburn. The equipment goes to Columbus, Georgia, while the equipment crew must fly to Montgomery, Alabama, then drive to Columbus to get it. Ronnie, Sam, and The Boys get an ancient chartered plane to Columbus. It's a four-hour flight, and after takeoff they find there is no food, no drink, and no cigarettes on board, plus no heat and stuck-open vents under every seat that emit steady arctic winds.

Dallas-Auburn was the low point and everyone was bitching. Mick wanted Bill Belmont "carpeted," and Bill said the crew thought the Stones were "a bunch of snobs playing dull music." Rookie Mick Taylor was bewildered, and Stew, on every Stones tour since they were doing England's cinema circuit, was disgusted. "We used to just do a bleeding tour," he said in soft Scots, "get into town, get a room, hire a few local blokes to carry the gear, set up and do the gig—thirty, forty cities like that. But when you start hiring whole houses and cars and have people like Ronnie Schneider and *John Jaymes,* for Godsakes, around, you're bound to have trouble."

The real problem, however, is not the disorganization as such, but the subtly pervasive hysteria that comes with being close

164

to the Rolling Stones. The Stones are *stars*—on tour, if not else-where—automatically the center of attention and privilege. None insist on that status, but they accept its security with an equanimity both innocent and arrogant.

The Stones' perspective on the tour is, of course, unique. They are, for instance, the only people who have old friends along for company—themselves. The whole machine with all its delicate tunings is caused by and devoted to them; their only job is to play. Since they do that well, they are willing to treat the rest as someone else's job and thus ignore it. All shy and private people, they retreat as best they can from the center of attention. Charley, like all drummers, is just the drummer; one suspects that he has opinions, but he keeps them to himself. Bill Wyman, always followed closely by Astrid, goes his own silent way; Mick Taylor, although always treated with a generous courtesy by the others, is still, by virtue of his newness, on his own. Keith, the group's *eminence bizarre,* and Mick's unsentimental alterego, scorns any overt leadership role. Only Jagger—to all non-Stones the very center of this hierarchical solar system—takes an active interest in the overall direction of the machine; yet he refuses to lead it, and so no one does. His wishes for it are vague and unformed; as interpreted by the loyal lieutenants, they become the ultimate command: "Mick wants. . . ." But when the organization broke down completely in Dallas, he complained bitterly that "The trouble with this tour is that there is no one strong enough to *run* it." The irony went unremarked; the Stones, and certainly Jagger, are the tour's essential premise, and therefore, if not always right, never wrong.

All non-Stones are relatively insecure and in a constant struggle to maintain their own egos and their place in the graded orbits around the Stones. While on one hand there is an under-current of hostility to the Stones—why do *they* always get the dope first?—there is a stronger one of self-dramatization, a pressure to maximize one's importance to the Stones. That in turn increases the Stone's status; everyone is more important if the Stones are more important.

John Jaymes's noisy finaglings in Oakland are a classic example of the syndrome, but almost no one is immune—Ronnie, for instance. A nephew of the Stones' business manager Alan Klein, he quit Klein's firm, ABKCO Industries, just before the tour and set up Stones Promotions Ltd. as an independent company. The Stones' tour manager when he worked for Klein, he now has cautious hopes of enlarging his role, if not of replacing Klein entirely. The best means to that end is a successful tour which in his terms means, above all, substantial profits. He can do nothing the Stones do not want, i.e., baseball stadium concerts, but he can drive exacting bargains. He does; he gets the whole guarantee from each promoter, rather than the normal half, before concert time. This he puts into short-term notes at 8½ percent. He cuts the booking agency's commission to 7½ percent; it is normally between 10 and 15 percent for major acts. At every concert he dogs the promoters, watching for every possible hustle, checking receipts, and bullying them when they complain of minor contract infractions. He makes sure the Stones know all of this in gleeful boasts of his prowess.

(It is not all boasting; Stones Promotions Ltd. grosses approximately $1.7 million on the tour. From that figure, however, must be deducted all costs and overheads, including the fees for Terry Reid, B. B. King, Ike and Tina, and Chuck Berry, all hired by the corporation. Each Stone probably added about $50,000 to his present fortune for the month's work.)

Sam makes himself gatekeeper to The Boys and treats them with a deference due only retarded royal children. Jo worries she cannot be all that Mick expects of her. Jeff, the equipment boy, quits Terry Reid to join the Stones because "carrying Stones' amps is more fun." For myself, a day spent close to the Stones is a "good day," one away from the inner circle a nervously boring drag. We all grow tired of smiling but fear stopping. The jostling of those close to the Stones to stay close is—entirely noncoincidentally—strikingly similar to the mad rush to the stage at every concert.

All of which is a colossal bummer, but the miracle is that, despite it and even with it, the tour is an absolute gas for all concerned. That is indubitably due to the Rolling Stones; the hysteria is but the obverse of the excitement, and the coin comes up heads far more often than tails. Withal we are mates and have great fun together. And night after night, the concerts themselves are a stoned perfect thrill and delight to the ear, eye, mind, and soul.

Girl: I LOVE the Rolling Stones.
Time Reporter: So do I, but . . .
Girl: No buts for me. Mick is so beautiful. You know how he
can stand there with his hand on his hip, twitching his little ass,
and then he smiles! and falls back, pushing the microphone
away, and does little hops, I could die.
Reporter: Wow, you really . . .
Girl: And Keith, he's so mean and sexy—evil, my girl friend
calls it, but I bet he's real shy inside. And Charley's got the
greatest smile, looks like a camel or a dolphin, or somebody who
knows just everything.
Reporter: I like them in my head, but I don't know how to
show it.
Girl: Well, take off your tie, stupid, and let it all hang out. That's
your story 'cause that's what the Stones are all about!

No two concerts are the same; each is influenced by an infinity of variables. The Champaign hall is open and spacious, Dallas's Moody Auditorium low-ceilinged and dense; the Arizona State Coliseum is a scarred old rodeo palace. On B. B. King nights the mood is subtly spiritual; Tina Turner nights are unmistakably musky. One concert influences the next. Tired, rested, stoned, unstoned, grooving, or edgy, the Stones themselves are never the same. Among other things, the Stones are Englishmen in America; they think the cars, papers, TV, freeways, clothes, slang, and even airport shops filled with the products of a thousand "fad merchandisers," are all far out and fascinating. Dallas, Alabama, Chicago—they get a buzz from just being in such exotic, storied places, and it all comes out in the music.

On the way to Fort Collins, Mick and Keith set the basic format, scribbling the names of fourteen tunes (out of thirty rehearsed) on airplane stationery. "Jumping Jack" to open, then Chuck Berry's "Carol" from their first record, "Sympathy for the Devil" and "Stray Cat Blues"—all uptempo rockers. Then Mick and Keith alone on two slow blues, "Prodigal Son" and "You Gotta Move," then the moving "Love In Vain" from their new album with the whole band. A little pickup with "Under My Thumb" and "I'm Free," then the showpiece, "Midnight Rambler," followed by another Berry tune, "Little Queenie," to open a string of their biggest hits, each building on the one before:

167

"Satisfaction," "Honky Tonk Woman," and "Street Fighting Man." Nicely balanced between old and new, fast and slow, the show has a solid dramatic form—strong opening, introspective middle, then out to a one-two-three finale.

They never stop changing the order and balance. "Love in Vain" moves forward to the spot before "Prodigal" so they can come out of the blues straight into "Thumb." That is sometimes replaced with "Gimme Shelter." "I'm Free" is dropped after Oakland, and they start doing "Live with Me." Mick fiddles with his costume, too; sometimes in white, he most often wears black pants with silver buttons from waist to heel, a long crimson scarf, a studded belt, and a black T-shirt with the upside-down U glyph of Leo, his sun sign. The format changes less than any other aspect of the concerts. "If we keep the same tunes," explains Keith, "we can improvise within them rather than stumbling rigidly through new ones all the time."

> Did you hear about the Midnight Rambler,
> Well, honey, it's no rock 'n' roll show,
> I'm talking about the Midnight Gambler,
> The one you never seen befo'.*
>
> MICK JAGGER-KEITH RICHARD

The concerts always improve. But there are down nights. In Auburn, Chuck Berry refuses to get off the stage doing his night club routine on "Ding a Ling," and the hall is full of Southern fraternity gentlemen and their ladies. The Stones concert is a prestige date: Friday night the Stones, then drive to Athens Saturday to see the Auburn Tigers play the Georgia Bulldogs. They sit there in their Ivy League suits and permanent waves, still trying to catch up with 1959. Maybe high school kids would have a better time, but they're all watching their own night football games. All over America kids are learning they can be teenagers at thirty-five, but the Auburn crowd is a comfortable thirty-five at twenty-one. When the second show closes at 2:00 A.M., student entertainment director Jette Campbell announces, "The Dean of Women Students has said all girls have 'when over' permission, so don't worry about being late." It gets the biggest applause of the night.

But no, I cannot describe the shows for you, nor tell you what fun they were, nor explain the breathtaking symmetry of Chip Monck's blue spotlights cutting icelike down through the smoky air to end in golden sparkles on Charley's cymbals in the pool of red-green light that is the stage. What *is* that rush that inevitably comes as Bill Wyman's bass makes its guttural run to open "Live with Me" and Mick picks it up with those masterfully slimy lines, "Well, I got real nasty habits, yeah, an' I take my tea at three." Or the kaleidoscopic flash of memories of times and dances and girls when they get to "Little Queenie"—"She's too cute to be a minute over seventeen." Every night, sometimes with "Jumping Jack's" first note, sometimes not until Keith steps forward to do his solo on "Sympathy," Stanley Booth (a remarkable lunatic from Memphis) and I share a look of bewildered joy, know we are both *insane* Rolling Stones fans, and then whoop with the jolts of pleasure they give us.

They are a *band,* the Rolling Stones, five young men working together to make that precious, precious thing that is rock 'n' roll music—no "type" of rock, just rock 'n' roll, period. Keith, their master musician and leader of the band, looks strikingly like Isak Dinesen in her old age. The resemblance is more than skin deep. Every night he plays his lean and keening lines, and beneath their harshness there appears suddenly a dedication to the classic elements of music—form, clarity, and grace—so intense that his wasted face, pathetic skinniness, and utter carelessness for his body will never be a mystery again. He sits to play "You Gotta Move," and his hands bring from the battered steel guitar a lyric twinging sadness and crushingly fateful chords. As Charley keeps a muffled beat behind them, Mick sings the ancient Negro words—

> You may be high, you may be low,
> You may be rich, chile, you may be po',
> But when the Lord gets ready,
> You gotta move.
> You see that woman, she walk the street,
> You see the police on his beat,
> Now when the Lord gets ready,
> You gotta move.*

and you know that they know exactly what it means. Arrogant

*"YOU GOTTA MOVE" by Robert Johnson.

they may be, but their absolute knowledge of that rock-bottom blues truth gives them full right to a cynical disdain for those who haven't dared to learn it.

Interviewers ask Mick Taylor if it feels strange to replace Brian Jones, and he never knows what to stay. Of course it is strange, and Mick, with his shy and friendly face, has not replaced him. But only those who ask care. His playing gets stronger. On "Sympathy" and "Love in Vain" he shares solo spots with Keith, and by Champaign we are all listening to what he has to say—a music quieter and less sure of itself than Keith's, but fresher, more open and searching. The spontaneous applause that greets his work is full welcome to the group.

Bill and Charley—the rhythm section. Not very fancy, almost dull. Bill stands there like a gargoyle, his eyes blank and his fingers barely seeming to move over his baby blue Fender, one of the cheapest basses you can buy. Charley keeps the beat and does his job as if he were a musician they had hired for the night. And yet you can't *listen* to the Stones without moving, without succumbing to their dark and merciless drive. Thank Bill and Charley for that inescapable pounding that grounds each song to a dynamo.

"I'm free to sing my song, even though it's out of tune" —Mick Jagger wrote those words as a twenty-year-old boy, and prancing and nancing up there in the middle of his starburst, he lives them. Leo is the lion's sign, the sign of the full golden sun of summer, of radiant self-love, and Mick is Leo incarnate. Dancer and singer, he does not interpret his songs bodily like James Brown, but moves in independent counterpoint. He ducks, leaps, and almost falls; stamps his foot, then suddenly is still; bends out over the edge of the stage or walks petulantly away and gulps beer with his back to the crowd. He can flirt, scorn, mock, and beseech, changing mood and aspect with a dazzling and magical speed. At times he seems less himself than his archetype, the beautiful young man—Narcissus, Patroclus, David, Romeo— that ideal creature of myth beloved by all generations of men and women. Just barely graceful, erotic more than sexy, and only now becoming truly handsome, he is *free*. It seems the only word ("He does anything he wants," someone behind me murmurs in Dallas as we watch, transfixed): free as a bird, free form, free time, and fancy free. Free to sing his song, any old time.

170

Then all together—the combination of the sight and sound is mind-boggling. There is in the show some reference to all the arts, painting and sculpture as well as dance and drama. Mick and Keith, Keith and Charley, Bill and Charley, Keith and Mick Taylor; the empathetic intricacy of their relationships as they bend to one another, listen, suggest, take command, retreat, form, re-form; and all the time the lights are changing, and the terribly familiar songs are turning up new lines, new associations, until one can only bathe unreflectingly in it all.

And the Stones, of course, are but half the concert. The kids, 10,400 at Fort Collins, 36,000 in LA, 19,318 in Oakland, 21,000 in Chicago—thousands and thousands and thousands of kids—are the other half, and are they ever fine! Of all the concert variables they are the most important. Nothing can happen without them, but with them, when they start to smile and shake, to stand and shout, to forget why they came and how they got there and what they were planning to do the next day, to forget everything but being *right there,* then everything happens, and it's no longer a concert, but a wild high-time happiness that everyone shares.

There's a million theories about rock 'n' roll, what it is and means, but what's most obvious is most overlooked: it's music. Plain old music; rhythm, melody, and harmony; mathematical relationships of frequencies and time intervals; those pleasing combinations of vibrations that some philosophers declare to be the ultimate mystery and reality of the universe. And these kids, ordinary American kids we all know and recognize, are true music lovers. They just love it, that's all; spend vast sums on it, listen to hours of it, think about it incessantly, find their heroes among its makers, date their lives by it and, in geometrically increasing numbers, make it themselves. When I was in school, musical kids were the sissies, and we read in social studies that Italy was a musical country. What is going on here anyway? The Holy Rollers used to be a minority sect.

In Phoenix three girls are sitting in the front row, obviously friends who came together: a pretty girlish blonde, a rather plain brunette with glasses and a cool beauty-queen type who smokes her cigarettes in a holder. No dates. At first they are reserved and stiff, trying to look their best—do they have fantasies that maybe *He* will notice them? They smoke a lot. The blonde starts to smile during "Carol"; the brunette blushes when Mick puts the microphone between his thighs on "Sympathy." She recovers during the blues, but the beauty-queen's jaw sags open the tiniest bit. Her tongue flickers out during "Under My Thumb" and she drops her holder. She doesn't pick it up. By this time the blonde's neatly coiled hair has somehow come undone on one side and, never taking her eyes off the stage, she vainly pecks at it with one hand. "Midnight Rambler" is too much for all of them. In its moment of eerie silence they watch as Mick slips off his belt and falls to his knees. He raises it above his head.

Well, now, you've heard about the Boston . . .

Bam! The belt comes down as the band hits a monster chord. The blonde almost falls back over her seat, the brunette covers her breasts and the beauty-queen goes limp. Mick hisses.

Honey, he ain't one of those!

They're hooked. No more cigarettes. The brunette's glasses have disappeared, and when the lights go on, they're on their feet. Tears start in the blonde's eyes. The stage rush begins, and a big hulking kid leaps over three rows, aiming for a gap beside the beauty-queen. He doesn't make it and hits her heavily on the shoulder. She doesn't feel a thing. Her body rolls with the unexpected blow as if she were water. I lose them in the crowd; my last glimpse is the brunette, her hands above her head, palms up and fingers spread wide, her mouth wide open, singing, "No satisfaction, baby, no satisfaction," and she is beautiful now, transformed, her eyes bright as a bride's, her hair swinging loose around her shoulders.

Faces pop out of the crowd, eyes suddenly make contact, and for a few seconds, kids who may be twenty rows apart and total strangers, smile, wave, and dance together. Kids with beards, kids with mustaches; twelve-year-olds with their parents, thirteen-year-old runaways; kids stoned on acid, kids who've never touched a joint; unimaginable freaks and student body presidents. In the top balconies where the Stones are barely visible but the music still bell-clear, kids dance in the aisles behind their seats as if the concert were just the best sock-hop ball in the world. There are no bad dancers; the straightest-looking kids move with awesome grace, picking up on the songs at whatever level they dig best and working it on out. Some kids look scared, afraid to show what they feel, and they watch it all happen, holding their jackets and handbags tight in damp hands. But they're not having a *bad* time, and who knows what they'll do at the next concert?

They seem the children of some miracle. I have, I suppose, no real knowledge of who they are and what they'll become. What it *means* I could never say. Maybe it is as illusory as music itself, some hypnotic trick, an evening's diversion, but I do know that while I am dancing too, and singing along with "Satisfaction" until my lungs are bursting, I feel a kinship with these kids, my brothers and sisters, as profound and happy as any I have ever known . . .

> *We're gonna find some satisfaction,*
> *Gonna get us a little satisfaction,*
> *Gonna find some,*
> *Gonna get some,*
> *Some satisfaction,*
> *Some satisfaction,*
> *Satisfaction,*
> *Satisfaction baby,*
> *Some satisfaction.*

Dearest Mick I, Mick II, Keith, Charley, and Bill,

Welcome back to America and Chicago. It's been a long time since I saw you last. Never in my life have I ever missed your concerts. Even if you gave two shows I would spend the whole day with you and enjoy every heart breaking minute.

I'm very sorry to hear about Brian. I'm a Roman Catholic and I gave Brian two spiritual bouquets. Masses are being said for Jones in America now. One bouquet in Chicago and one in Michigan, I promise that as soon as I feel I have the money I will give you all a bouquet. There are Masses also for the living. At different times I will be sending you Mass cards c/o your fan club c/o Jo Bergman. I want to help you people. I'm so worried about you and I luv you so much.

I do hope you enjoy my cookies that I made for you. They all were made each with luving care my dears. If I get my gift and letter thru would you if you can give me some acknowledgement that you received my letter etc. all in one piece? I still have your last letter that I got from you in 1965. I got it on May 11 and you had a concert May 10 I think Mother's Day. That concert was really great. I luv all of your concerts very much. Your records are the greatest. They make me feel good all over whenever I play them, but lately I feel a little sad.

Anyway would it be possible if you could send a heart-broken, lonely girl 21 yrs old fan a word of encouragement, and acknowledgement of my gift. Thank you.

I can't sleep tonight. It's now almost 12:45 A.M. I wish somebody with real strong hands would rub my back real hard and good. I've been having back aches now for about two weeks straight. They hurt like anything. Oh well, I wish I were real tired too, but I'm not.

Well better go. Take care and may Our Lord always watch over you and protect you especially while you're touring and crossing the ocean going from country to country. Do be good Stones and let me hear from you. I'm so lonely.

All My Luv. Always My Dears,
(Signed)

(A letter attached to a plate of cookies given the Stones in Chicago. The Stones neither saw the letter nor had any of the cookies.)

Abbie Hoffman is at the Chicago concert (along with the most and loudest-screaming girls of any show). He didn't have a ticket but an usher who recognized his face and curly hair let him in to the $7.50 section right up front. He had been trying to reach the Stones for days, even calling up the Ambassador West and pretending to be Elvis ("Yassuh, I jes' wanned to see how Mick an' the boys were doin' "). He sends a note to the Stones from his seat; it gets through. Mick wants to see him too, and they get together in the dressing room for a few minutes before show time.

Mick is dressing and brushing his hair; both are a little awkward. They compliment each other on what they've been doing. "Your thing is sex, mine's violence," says Abbie, and they both crack up. Abbie asks if he knows that they are playing at the site of the 1968 Democratic convention. "Sure I know," says Mick.

"Anita and I just came from the Washington Moratorium," says Abbie. "Great. There was Mitch Miller, or maybe it was Pete Seeger, leading the crowd in 'Give Peace a Chance.' "

"Why not," says Mick.

"I'll give peace a chance," says Abbie laughing, "one more chance."

A joint comes by and they have a few tokes. Abbie wanders over to Ronnie, who is reading contracts.

"Hey, man, you the cat to see about money?"

Ronnie looks up guardedly at this freak in the inner sanctum.

"See, we could use some bread for our trial, you know, the Chicago 8. I promise I'll pay you back right after it's over."

"No," says Ronnie with utter unconcern. Abbie goes back to Jagger.

"Could you lend us some money for our trial? It's expensive making the revolution."

"We got our own trials," says Mick. He slips on his deerskin moccasins. Abbie is left hanging. None of the other Stones seem to know or care who he is. Mick Taylor asks him for a match.

"Bunch of cultural nationalists," he says good-humoredly as he goes out the door. After the concert he says he's not sure how the Stones fit into the revolution, but "Mick Jagger

176

sure is something else on stage." In a speech a few weeks later he calls him "our Myra Breckinridge."

With Chicago down and the tour more than half done, the Stones fly back to Los Angeles for a week's break. The first day back is for taping the Ed Sullivan show. "We wanted to do Sullivan, not one of the new shows, 'cause there's nothing more far out than the Ed Sullivan Show," says Keith. "It's so old it's funky." Like Ed himself, whom all the technicians in CBS's huge Hollywood studio call "Dad." The taping should be a bore—the band standing in place faking it to a record while Mick sings a new vocal track—but Dad saves the day.

Between numbers he is supposed to walk up to Mick, say a few words, and then retire while they begin the next tune. Out he lumbers as they finish "Gimme Shelter."

"That was great, Mick, glad to have you back on the show. What are you going to sing now?"

"We're going to ..."

But Ed, in suit, shirt, and tie of television blue, is so precisely what he has always been and always will be, that Mick starts to laugh. Keith howls and runs to hide behind the silver foil set. The audience titters.

"Cut," someone cries, and they try again. Ed says exactly the same words with exactly the same inflection, and this time everyone laughs.

"Maybe we ought to do it without you saying anything," Mick suggests, trying to be both practical and kind. That's okay with Ed. Third try. But Ed forgets not to say anything and again delivers his lines. The place erupts with laughter. Fourth time gets it, and the Stones disappear for a week of rest far from the madding crowd and public eye.

Cathy: Two years ago my girl friend Mary and I were married and living in Ojai. It was okay, but boring, and all we ever thought about was Mick Jagger. We loved him a lot more than our husbands. So one day we decided: we'll split, get divorces, and move down to the Strip. It was great, you know, hanging around the clubs. We got to know a lot of groups but never forgot Mick. So imagine how we felt in the Whisky one night when this guy said he was Sam Cutler and asked if we'd

177

like to be with the Stones when they were in LA, and drive 'em around and stuff.

It was Sam who picked me up, and I felt loyal to him, but when we were up at Mick's house the first night—well, I'm only human. We were all sitting around, and Mick said he was going to bed. I was really disappointed. But he came down again and started pouring perfume on me, and sort of whispered, "Will you come up with me, then." I almost died, but I managed to say, "Only if my friend Mary can come too." We had been together through two years, and had made a pact not to leave the other out. He said okay.

It was funny, man, I could hardly get it on. He makes all the sexy noises in bed, like he does singing. I was laughing so hard, but know what was funniest? For two years I had been thinking with every guy, "He's great, but he's not Mick Jagger." And then with Mick, all I could think was, "He's great, but he's not Mick Jagger."

He has to work at being Mick Jagger, you know? Some mornings he wakes up and says, "I feel so fragile this morning, Cathy, be gentle," and I think, "This is the Mick I idolized?" But now I know he's a person I love him more.

Anyway I'm having the time of my life. I mean it.

A black lady cabdriver takes me in from the airport to the Detroit concert, the first after the break, and tells me she thinks it's great, all these kids getting together for music. "It was the same when I was that age," she says. "I'd save up all my pennies, sneak out of the house if I had to, to hear Charley Barnett. You might think he's square, but back then it was the greatest. The way I look at it is, it's all jumpin' music, and ain't nobody ever gonna stop kids from lovin' jumpin' music."

In Motor City it is jumping music indeed. The Stones play better than ever, and the kids are dynamite. Some places the kids seem to be imitating San Francisco, New York, or LA, but in Detroit they have a funky independence: unwashed, tough, but cheery. Crazy-leaping before the stage, they're laughing at the Stones because that night it seems so *funny,* and the Stones dig them back, spreading out the songs, adding choruses, and building finales until it looks like they might just play all night.

But no; run off, roar out and into a tiny plane that drones us across a bed of moonlit clouds to New York. Bill and Astrid fall asleep, Charley and Mick Taylor stare calmly out the windows, and Mick, Keith, and Ronnie play poker on a drum case. Dozens of joints make their mellow rounds, and conversation drops to the chatter from the card game.

Keith plays, Mick plays to win, and Ronnie plays to win money, but they are three close friends, and no one really cares. Ronnie makes like a hot-time dealer ("Pair of deuces on my left, possible straight on the right, and not a thing in my hand, bet up gentlemen"). Mick and Keith play back like titled English ladies at *fin de siecle* Monte, broken by fortune but haughty to the end.

"I'll stake my carriage," says Keith, adjusting an imaginary stole.

"My horses and one chambermaid on this turn of cards, sirrah," says Mick.

"Are you kidding me?" says Ronnie. His wad of bills is held neatly in his hand; Mick's and Keith's are crumpled heaps before them. "Okay, I'll throw in my mother and my uncle."

"And no children?" says Lady Keith, horrified.

'Sure, my kid too," says Ronnie. "Another card, ladies."

It goes on like that until the clouds melt away. The lights of Manhattan are bright beneath us. The plane floats into the LaGuardia Marine Terminal and the droning stops. In the sudden silence we straggle across the wet, black macadam. It's about 4:00 A.M. Our only greeters are the limousine drivers shivering in the cold. The Cadillacs purr through Queens, over the bridge and on, through streets now oyster grey, to the Plaza. On little cat feet, as it were, the Rolling Stones arrive in New York.

An elegant New York groupie—a veritable Madame Pompadour at the high court of the counter culture—arranges an intimate party for the Stones in a Village apartment. By invitation only, and there are only thirty-five invitations. It's very late and very stoned. The guests, all young, all long-haired, sit or stand around the edges of the room, silent and nearly motionless, ultra-cool and ultra-awkward. No one knows what to say, for over there in a little group are the two Micks and Keith. A blues record is on, and they're chatting about it softly among them-

179

selves. When they get too tired, they leave. It's the only real party the Stones attend in New York, and when the gossip mills get rolling the next afternoon as the in-crowd awakes, it's considered high points to have been there.

New York and Los Angeles are as different on tour as they are at any time. Gone is the open, lazy feeling of the Coast; the four-walls feeling of hotel life replaces it. The idea of the Plaza is a gas, but as daily fact it is just another hotel. Bizarrely expensive, the Plaza stops its room service at 1:00 A.M. (lunch time for this crew), and the service is slower than the slowest "Squaliday Inn." A sandwich and a beer is an hour wait, an elevator five minutes, and a phone call to another room a succession of "One moment, please's." The cast again adds extras: cops, drivers, reporters, petitioners of every sort, buddies of John Jaymes, and then buddies of buddies.

Suite 969, the Plaza, afternoon. Ronnie, tie off, feet up, is on the phone. "What about overage in Illinois? Yeah, Champaign? . . . Whaddya mean, late? We closed the show on time, didn't we? . . . I don't care what the man said. *I* said, not him." A shirtless John Jaymes, his chest, back, and enormous belly covered with hair, is on another line. "Yeah, I know a lotta people were promised interviews. Pope Paul, he was promised an interview, but he can't make it. Sorry, man, no show."

Four beefy security men, Italian friends of John's from the Bronx, sit around a table playing poker. In the bedroom Cecil Beaton paces about as an assistant snaps pictures of Mick. Beaton's silvered voice drifts out into the sitting room: "Great . . . great . . . excellent, marvelous . . great . . . lower and spin . . . great . . . yes, oh, yes . . . great." A Daily News reporter waits patiently for the interview he is never going to get. A pretty young model named Barbara, soon to take John's body-painting kit on a nationwide tour ("my big break"), plays solitaire. Jo's on another phone to London but stops to rummage through her bag when Sam dashes in to borrow her hair dryer for Mick Taylor. "I want it back this time," says Jo.

"Sure, luv," says Sam, "and do you have any perfume for Keith?"

"What kind does he like?"

"*Joy,*" says Sam. "He puts it in his bleeding armpits."

Mike Quatro, the pint-sized twenty-three-year-old Detroit promoter, kibbitzes the card game. A child prodigy piano player on Lawrence Welk, he's got a house in Grosse Point Farms from the proceeds of his rock 'n' roll agency—promotion firms. He's in management too, his biggest act being the Hedonists, an all-girl group made up of his four older sisters. He's come to New York hoping to make future deals with Ronnie, deals that might affect his plans for doing some "Woodstock-type" festivals next summer. Ronnie gets off the phone, and Mike slides over to him. "How about talking business, Ronnie?"

"Sure, kid, but listen, Mike, will you call room service again for those goddam sandwiches."

"Sure thing," says Mike, leaping to the phone.

Around this crowded center is the New York "scene," which, from its own center at Max's Kansas City, plots incessantly on how either to infiltrate the Stone's center or at least to find out "what's happening." Max's hears that there are code names used to reach the Stones' rooms; that this supergroupie or that supergroupie has or has not made it to Mick or Keith; that Charley is sick; that if Jimi Hendrix decides to go to X's party, Bill Wyman will probably be there too; and that perhaps, hope of hopes, the Stones will come to Max's itself.

The scenesters (a New Yorker once called them "the young elite of the communications industry") finally get a chance to see their heroes at the obligatory press conference held in the Rockefeller Center's Rainbow Room, sixty-five stories above the ground. At no concert has there been such hysteria. Photographers and TV crews and reporters with tape machines press forward to the microphone-loaded table with a loudmouthed aggression that the Kodak-wielding kids in Dallas or Chicago would have found appalling. Young "rock writers," "company freaks" and scenemakers who have been ringing PR lady Doreen for days to get there, sip their drinks and tell their friends that it's such a bore. The Stones file in to a blinding splatter of flashbulb explosions. Everyone cries for everyone else to sit down. All stay standing.

Sam introduces the Stones by name.

"Can we have that again?" shouts a TV man.

"Down in front!"

"Shut up willya so we can hear."

Keith: "Should we scream at you like you scream at us?"

Silence. There are no questions.

Mick: "We're just sitting here, man, *you* gotta do it."

An interminable statement-question on marijuana legalization and on violence. Mick says something like "we gotta stop the fight between young people and their . . ." before he's cut off. What about the USA?

Mick: ". . . it just explodes all the time, it's great, you look more beautiful than ever over here."

You wrote "Satisfaction"; are you more satisfied now?

Mick: ". . . sexually satisfied, financially unsatisfied, philosophically still trying . . ."

Keith: "Wiser, wiser."

Sadder?

Keith: "No, of course not."

What about John Lennon giving back his MBE?

Keith: "At last! He should never have taken it. We don't care, we'll never get one."

Hey, Mick, you were wearing an omega button in LA. It stands for draft resistance. How do you feel about that?

Mick: "Draft resistance? I though it stood for infinity."

What about being philosopher king?

Mick: "I withdraw from the role, it's a banality."

Bill and Charley are asked no questions and say nothing. Mick Taylor is asked about taking Brian's place. He smiles back at the questioner, then looks away.

"That's it," says Sam.

Mick: "Thank you, New York."

The consensus on the packed elevators is that it was a freak show, but then everyone knew it would be, and knew they should have stayed home.

New York is disappointed. It had wanted the Stones to be the Stones of the days when the pop demimonde was taking over the columns from the café society that had run itself down twisting at the Peppermint Lounge; when Andy and Baby Jane and pill parties on the Lower East Side were the action. But this Thanksgiving weekend Max's is full of PR men, not painters, and the Stones are five young men who have been away from home for a month and a half, and who want to see friends and family, not new streams of strangers, however glamorous.

Charley and Keith call home to London every day, and when one girl gets to Keith's room, he offers her tea and shows her baby pictures. Mick Taylor just wishes he could find a few hours to walk about the city and shop. Bill and Astrid do go downtown to see a strip show ("I'd never seen one," says Astrid, "and, oh, but she was fat!"), and Charley slips off to Slugs to hear the Tony Williams Lifetime, but otherwise it's sleep and work. Jo gets them together to discuss what concerts and TV dates to do when they return to England, Mick calls Ahmet Ertegun of Atlantic Records to ask permission to use their studios in Muscle Shoals, Alabama, and Keith never stops writing songs.

They are *doing* the tour now, still as brilliantly as ever, but there are no more surprises; Philadelphia, Baltimore, three shows at the Garden, and then Boston—the concerts are now a perfect machine. The record they were finishing in Los Angeles, *Let It Bleed* (a pun on the Beatles *Let It Be*), is a smash hit, and the crowds cheer the new tunes as much as they do the old.

In Philly I see a dozen kids charge one door, knock down the elderly ticket-taker, and scatter into the crowd. An SDS pack in Beantown's ancient Boston Garden rips down the American flag and then is trapped and beaten by quick-moving police. John Jaymes sprains his wrist when he tries to bash one of the kids and hits a wall instead.

Madison Square Garden is dotted with semicelebrities: an aging Murray the K, promoter of the Stones' first American concert ("they were scared little boys back in '64"), a tipsy Janis Joplin who joins Tina Turner for a brief but ecstatic moment that brings the house down, and a subdued Jimi Hendrix who jams with Keith in the dressing room. Leonard Cohen, Paul Simon, Woody Allen, Viva, and the Jefferson Airplane all come to see what it is all about. They record the Garden shows, Glyn Johns hunched over a Wally Heider sixteen-track machine in a Hertz truck backstage. Glyn wants a double album of everybody—Terry Reid, B. B., and Ike and Tina—if they can get contract releases. Mick doesn't like the idea. "Double albums are so pompous; Dylan's is the only one I could ever stand." Bob Dylan, though, doesn't come to the Garden. "He doesn't do this kind of thing anymore," says a friend. "He's a family man, doesn't want to be a star making a fuss."

The tour is coming to an end. After Baltimore, Ronnie starts a countdown. Leaving Boston Garden, he shouts, "Only one more to go!"

"I don't believe it," says Charley, "they really want us to go home, Ronnie and John do. It was fun at first, then work, now a bloody drag to have us around."

"That's right," says Ronnie. "Go home, you little limey."

"I will," says Charley, "will do."

At 3:00 A.M. a seemingly endless and disorderly stream of very drunk young men and women of New York society comes flowing through the lobby of the Plaza. They've been at a ball at which twelve of their kind have come out from nowhere into what their mothers at least must consider Somewhere. The boys are in white tie and tails or modish varieties of evening dress, the girls in awesomely beautiful formal gowns. Few of them are out of their teens. One tries to slide down a brass stair railing. When he falls off, his mates cheer him with loud hip, hip, hooray's. Five boys stagger along, their arms around each other's shoulders, trying to recall, then sing, that World War I song about "Rinky dinky parley voo." An astonishing vision: children of the fifties, consciously acting out, on the cusp of the seventies, a perfect imitation of the twenties.

In walk the Rolling Stones et al, tired and disheveled from a hard night's work in Boston. Our stream passes theirs; the Stones take no notice, but a few of the Golden Youth stop and stare.

"Well, what do you know, the Rolling Stones!"

"In the Plaza? Ha, ha ha."

"You're Mick, aren't you, 'Satisfaction' and all?"

To some the Stones are just a bunch of hippies who have inexplicably swum into view, and a few V signs are flashed.

I stop to watch, and a pretty girl named Connie smiles and gives me a flower from her bouquet—is that etiquette when confronted by a long-hair? Two of her friends—Lyle in a floppy blue velvet bow-tie, and a dark Harvard freshman—stop, and we all talk for a few minutes.

The three apologize profusely not only for having been at the party, but also for their whole lives, then point out that they really are high society. "The nitty-gritty," says Lyle. Yes, they say, life's a bore, but amusing. The joints and the amyl nitrite poppers at the party were almost as plentiful as the champagne, they say, and some kids were even sniffing spoons of cocaine. Connie: "It's expensive, but *so* groovy if you can afford it" —which I am sure she can. Does she know that low class rock 'n' rollers like Mike Jagger and Bob Dylan have written songs to her?

"Oh, yes," she says. " 'Playing with Fire' is my favorite Stones song, and 'Just Like A Woman' my Dylan favorite. You know the line in it, 'her fog, her amphetamine, and her pearls'? Every time I hear it, I think, yeah, that's me. It feels pretty weird, I'll tell you."

> *...We're gonna vent our frustration,*
> *If we don't, we're gonna blow a 50-amp fuse.*
> MICK JAGGER-KEITH RICHARD

The last day of the tour is a wintry grey day in New York. We clear out of the Plaza and drive to the Marine Terminal to leave as we arrived. But we are late for the chartered plane to West Palm Beach, and so, we are told, must wait for new takeoff clearance. We wait. One hour goes by, then two. John and Ronnie dash angrily back and forth between plane and terminal. First they report engine trouble. Then a snow flurry, then President Nixon landing in Air Force One. Four hours, five hours.

After three hours all diversions have been used up. Charley wakes up to find the plane unmoved. Bill Wyman quits his card game with Al the security man and tries to sleep. Mick and Keith have run through all their tape cassettes. The Sunday paper is scattered all over the plane, and no one has missed skimming a month-old Sports Illustrated. There is nothing new to bitch about. They had planned to play at sundown, and it's already dark. Keith goes to sleep. We munch sandwiches, drink beer, and chat. I tell Mick about Connie and her favorite songs. "We make music to please all kinds," he says. "One of those kids said to me, 'You want to go to a debutante party,' and I said to him, 'There are no *real* debutantes in America.' "

Somehow a few of us start on politics, and for an hour carry on with the normal sound and fury. Bill goes back to his

185

cards; Mick Taylor never joins in. Like all such conversations, it is filled with unreal rhetoric and impossible hopes. We go round in circles, all wanting some indefinable "more" and having no idea how to find it. Sam's the organization man; it should be possible, he says, to get enough people together to seize a section of London.

"But what'll you do with it when you've got it?" asks Charley.

"Just run it the way *we* want to run it," says Sam, "whatever comes of it. We can't do worse than the bastards in power now."

"I think we should too," says Mick, "but in England you never will. Nobody's interested. In America there is at least a sense of change, people willing to try things, but England's dead."

"What do you want to knock off the old thing for when you've got nothing to take its place?" says Charley.

"I'd put *nothing* in its place," Mick shouts. "Just subvert it, do away with it because it's irrelevant and should be wiped out. But in England people *like* the system. With our so-called socialism, you couldn't believe the rules we've got, and people obey them just like they did the aristocracy. I wish things were *more* capitalistic, and less restrained."

"I don't know," says Charley, by now the only quiet voice. "I like my house and horses and land."

"You're nothing but a bleeding liberal, joining all the Preservation societies," says Sam.

"Another Cockney turned English gentleman," says Mick.

"I'll admit I'm materialistic," says Charley.

Sam corners Charley and runs down statistics on land use and population, and the conversation falls dead. "I'd do anything political I thought would work," Mick puts in as a parting shot, "that would really shake things, but I still haven't found anything as good as what I'm doing, or anybody to do it with."

By 10:00 P.M.—almost eight hours late—we're off the ground, for some reason in another plane. Mick had almost decided to call it off. "We could send a helicopter down there with the money and drop it on the crowd." By 1:00 A.M. we land in Florida, and after a few helicopter rides and another long wait in

186

a beachfront hotel, we get to the dragstrip and those cheering kids.

The Stones come on wrapped in jackets, but when Keith sees the crowd he strips his off in witness and plays in a skimpy shirt that leaves his stomach bare. He plays like a demon, fighting the cold that stiffens his fingers and de-tunes his guitar. The others, even Mick, look like they want to do a quick set and split, but Keith pushes them on. After "Sympathy," Mick apologizes for being late. "May we be forgiven?" he asks with a smirk. It's not good enough, and Keith cuts him off and starts "Stray Cat." Mick seems to get the message and steps forward to speak at the next break.

"We think it's really amazing to be here, you and us," he calls out, "because to get this all together after all the hassles and find you all here at four in the morning, is fantastic."

There's a small burst of cheers. Mick waves for silence. He is dead serious.

"You're all pretty special people, yes you are, and this moment is pretty special. It *matters* that you are here, but I guess you know it matters, because you stayed through the night, and you're here. We're all here."

For the first time since Oakland he calls for "I'm Free," and the kids are dancing as best they can. What lights there are go on the audience, and now, bathed in orange, they at least look warmer. Chip Monck, his long blond hair plastered down by intercom earphones, stops jumping to the music for a moment, and shouts a command into his mike. The spotlights on the high towers suddenly swing from the stage and swoop over the crowd, catching briefly, as if in deep blue pools, hundreds of happily shrieking kids.

The band builds to the finale which is now the finale of finales. It is almost a disaster. An amp blows out and is replaced. Mick Taylor breaks a string, Charley's hands are blue, and Mick keeps sniffling to clear his nose. Bill's bass is awesomely out of tune, and no one knows what the audience is hearing. But they drive on, Keith always taking the lead, and halfway through "Street Fighting Man," Chip, on some inspiration, calls again to the spotlight crews. The lights leave the crowd and turn to the sky, crossing and recrossing in triumphant arcs. Mick grabs the whole basket of rose petals and, not stopping for the normal handfuls, leans back and flings it as far as he can. Red petals are still falling as the last note dies away.

The helicopters take us back to the beach. In the east the sky is pink, and the night's clouds are disappearing to the west. The Stones walk to the water's edge and watch until streaks of crimson dart deep into the darkness, then, turning their backs, trudge to the hotel before the sun is fully risen. The chartered plane will take them to Muscle Shoals in a few hours and, forcing themselves to stay awake, they eat a desultory breakfast. John Jaymes comes over to the group of sofas and chairs where they are sprawled. He's carrying a 1970 Dodge catalogue and will, he says, take orders for whatever models they desire. It's all on Dodge and they can renew every year. They huddle excitedly to look at the catalogue, then give their orders as if John were a waitress in a hamburger joint: "I'll have mine silver, a hardtop," says Charley, "with the biggest engine and all the extras."

"And that includes air-conditioning, AM-FM radio and stereo tape deck," says John.

"Great," says Keith, "I'll have the same, but can I have lavender?"

John takes notes, makes a few suggestions, rechecks all the specifics, and walks away.

The Stones share a look that if not guilty is slightly furtive. Keith shrugs and laughs. Mick's eyes follow the wide sport-shirted back of his benefactor.

"Christ, I can't stand that man," he says with a condescending sneer.

> *I sung my song to Mr. Jitters,*
> *Yeah,*
> *And he said one word to me,*
> *And that was "death."*
>
> MICK JAGGER-KEITH RICHARD

They hit him . . . I couldn't tell whether it was a knife or not . . . but on the side of the head. And then . . . he came running towards me, and then fell down on his knees and then the Hell's Angel, the same one I was talking about, grabbed onto both of his shoulders and started kicking him in the face about five times or so, and then he fell down on his face, you know. . . . And then one of them kicked him on the side and he rolled over, and he

muttered some words. He said, "I wasn't going to shoot you."
We rubbed his back up and down to get the blood off so
we could see, and there was a big hole on his spine and a big
hole on the side and there was a big hole on his temple. A big open
slice. You could see all the way in. You could see inside. You
could see at least an inch down and stuff, you know. . . . All of us
were drenched in blood.

> *—An eyewitness account of the stabbing of eighteen-*
> *year-old Meredith Hunter, killed by Hell's Angels*
> *at Altamont. (From* Rolling Stone *Magazine.)*

It all came down at Altamont on that strange day. A
cold sun alternated with bright clouds, and 300,000 young Americans stepped into the future (or was it?), looked at each other,
and were frightened by what they saw. It was the biggest gathering in California (the population of San Francisco is 756,000)

since the Human Be-In three years before, not only in numbers but in expectation. In common with all the voluntary mass events of the sixties—was the Sproul Hall sit-in the first?—it would, all believed, advance the trip, i.e., reveal some important lesson intrinsic to and yet beyond its physical fact. The 300,000, all in unspoken social contract, came not only to hear music, but to bear living testimony to their own lives.

The Stones as well as the audience—and whether such a distinction should or could be made was one of the day's questions. They had wanted it to be in San Francisco's Golden Gate Park, their gift to the city and its culture. As their long hair, outrageous manners, and music had helped make San Francisco possible, San Francisco had helped make the past three years possible. Like thousands before them, the Stones were coming to say thank you. They hoped it would be in all senses a free concert, an event spiritually outside the commercial realm of the tour. It both was and was not. Neither the tour's footnote nor quite its denouement, that long Saturday was the drama's second and enigmatic ending which proved all endings as false and hard to mark as beginnings.

When the Stones left for Muscle Shoals, first Sam, then Jo, Ronnie and John, flew to San Francisco. Sam was met at the plane by Rock Scully, a long-time manager of the Grateful Dead, and concert planning began at the Dead's office and communal ranch. The Dead, hosts of more free concerts than any other band, are still the best embodiment of the San Francisco spirit that in 1967 captured the imagination of the world. True if harried believers in the psychedelic revolution, the Dead promised full cooperation (which they never gave the ill-fated Wild West), and the concert seemed to be in good if freaky hands. On Tuesday no site had been secured; by Wednesday morning the director of the Sears Point Raceway promised his grounds free of charge. Chip and his crew, aided by the Dead's extended family, started moving tons of equipment to the drag strip north of San Francisco. Then came the problems.

An essential element of free concerts is simplicity. You want to hear music? Okay, do it! Get a place, a source of power, a few flatbed trucks or a stage, a few bands, spread the word, trust to God, and have the thing. But this free concert was also a Stones concert, free or not, and everybody wanted a piece of the action. Hustlers of every stripe swarmed to the new scene like piranhas to the scent of blood.

The Sears Point man got cold feet or itchy palms or both and asked for six thousand dollars, plus five thousand dollars to be held in escrow against possible damages. Costs mounted on a dozen fronts; fearful of huge losses, Ronnie decided on a film designed for a TV special to be made by the Maysle brothers, who had already been shooting the final stages of the tour. Any profits would go to charity—"as yet unspecified," said John. The actual owners of the raceway, a Hollywood-based company called Filmways Corporation, which had promoted two of the town's concerts, heard about that and demanded film distribution rights as part of their fee. Ronnie refused, and Filmways, overriding their local management, responded by upping the fee to $100,000.

That was late Thursday. The San Francisco papers and radio stations were announcing Sears Point as the site, and a large volunteer vanguard had already encamped. That blatantly colorful attorney, Melvin Belli, offered his help in the fight with Filmways; Ronnie accepted it. The Dead office was abandoned as the HQ, and was replaced by Belli's office in San Francisco's financial district, and by Ronnie's suites in the posh Huntington Hotel. Managers of local bands started calling to get their groups on the stage for the priceless exposure; the city's rival Top-40 stations, KFRC and KYA, started running hourly bulletins, each trying to be the unofficial "Stones Station." Underground KSAN-FM, which had had the best coverage early in the week, was slowly edged out. Communes of ordinary hippies offering their services were rebuffed. The radical community, suspicious from the start, started talking about the festival as "one more shuck."

By midmorning Friday, Filmways was still adamant, but then got left when another track, this one a stock car oval called Altamont, offered its several hundred acres of rolling hills. Track director Dick Carter thought it would be "great publicity." The half-built stage at Sears Point was dismantled, and radio stations blasted the new directions with frantic assurances that, yes, the Stones concert was still on.

By late Friday afternoon the concert was the sole and obsessive topic of hip conversation, and Altamont a familiar name. KFRC had on-the-spot reporters on every spot worth being on, and KYA's DJ's bemoaned the fact that "some stations are trying to turn something that should be free and groovy into a commercial event." Both stations carried hi-fi store ads for "all new stereo tape recorders so *you* can make the Stones concert more than a memory." The scores of equipment trucks got to Altamont, fifty miles east of Berkeley, by early Friday evening; a huge volunteer crew worked like ants under blue floodlights amid a growing tangle of wires, planking and staging. "No one will be allowed on the grounds until 7:00 A.M. Saturday, so *stay home,*" was the broadcast word, but by midnight there were traffic jams miles from the site. The Stones got to the Huntington by ten, exhausted. In Alabama they had heard only the confusing rumors, but were determined to go ahead. "We'll have it in a bloody parking lot if we have to," said Keith. He and Mick flew out to see Altamont. Mick went back to get some sleep; Keith stayed all night.

As the stage crew labored, a few thousand people who had missed the roadblocks slept before the stage or stood by campfires; other thousands waited behind a fence for official opening time. I wandered from fire to fire; place was immediately made for any stranger, and joints steadily circled the impromptu hearths. I made scores of friends I'll never see again.

One girl told me solemnly that it would be a heavy day "because the sun, Venus, Mercury, and some other planet are all in Sagittarius, and the moon's on the Libra-Scorpio cusp." Another presented me with a grotesque doll made by her dead husband. "He lives in the doll; I know it," she said, nodding her head uncontrollably. "He sees everything." I said I was sorry. "Oh, that's okay, he was shot through the heart and lungs and the liver, but I really don't mind, 'cause he must have been meant to die, and anyway, I have the doll." Still nodding and smiling, she took it back and wrapped it in her shawl.

They came from everywhere. Two boys boasted that they had seen the Stones in LA, Chicago, Philly, and Palm Beach without ever buying a seat; someone countered by saying he had been to fourteen festivals plus Woodstock. A girl said she was from Akron, had run away to New Orleans, got an abortion in Houston, and had been on her way to Seattle ("I heard it's groovy there"), when she met a dealer in Phoenix who took her to San Francisco, then split to avoid a bust. "It's all so far out," she said. Somebody with a phonograph played *Abbey Road* over and over. The spindly light towers grew tall, generators roared, helicopters clattered overhead, and as night became grey dawn, Altamont

192

looked strikingly like the mad consummation of Fellini's *8½*.

At 7:00 A.M. the gates are opened. Over the hill and down into the hollow by the stage comes a whooping, running, raggle-taggle mob. From sleeping bags peer sleepy heads that duck back as the mob leaps over them and dashes between them. In minutes the meadow is a crush of bodies pressed so close that it takes ten minutes to walk fifty yards. Only the bravest blades of grass still peep up through the floor of wadded bedding. On and on comes the crowd; by ten it spreads a quarter mile back from the stage, fanning out like lichen clinging to a rock.

Rough beast, indeed; Yeats had it exactly:

> *. . . a vast image of* Spiritus Mundi
> *Troubles my sight: somewhere in the sands of the*
>   *desert*
> *A shape with lion body and the head of man,*
> *A gaze blank and pitiless as the sun,*
> *Is moving its slow thighs, while all about it*
> *Reel shadows of the indignant desert birds.**

There are the dancing beaded girls, the Christlike young men, and smiling babies familiar from countless stories on the "Love Generation," but the weirdos too, whose perverse and penetrating intensity no camera ever captures. Speed freaks with hollow eyes and missing teeth, dead-faced acid heads burned out by countless flashes, old beatniks clutching gallons of red wine, Hare Krishna chanters with shaved heads and acned cheeks. Two young men in filthy serapes and scraggly beards lean against a crushed and brightly painted derelict veteran of the Demolition Derby. In the brims of their cowboy hats are little white cards: "Acid $2." A shirtless black man stands in the center of a cheering circle. "I have in my hand," he barks, "one little purple tab of 100 percent pure LSD. Who wants this cosmic jewel?" A dozen hands reach out eagerly. "Who really wants it?" "I do, I do, I want it, me, me, me." "Going, going, gone to that freaky chick with the blue bandana." He tosses it to her, and reaches again into his leather bag. "I have in my hand one cap of mescaline, guaranteed organic. . . ."

Two middle-aged men with pinched Okie faces set up a

card table and hawk Rolling Stones programs left over from another tour. They've only sold a few when a milling crowd of radicals surrounds them. "It's free, man, nothing is sold today." "Better give the stuff away, man, or we'll rip it off in the name of the people." The men are frightened. A kid dashes up and grabs a handful of the glossy books. The table collapses. One man scoops the programs from the dirt, the other brandishes the table in wild-eyed defense. They retreat, walking backwards, as the brave guerrillas search for other targets.

Face by face, body by body, the crowd is recognizable, comprehensible. As ugly beautiful mass, it is bewilderingly unfamiliar—a timeless lake of humanity climbing together through the first swirling, buzzing, euphoric-demonic hours of acid. Is this Bosch or Cecil B. DeMille; biblical, medieval, or millenial? Are we lost or found? Are we *we,* and if we are, who are we?

Whoever or whatever, we are *here, all* here, and gripped by the ever-amazing intensity of psychedelics, we *know* that this being here is no accident but the inevitable and present realization of our whole lives until this moment. One third of a million postwar boom babies gathered in a Demolition Derby junkyard by a California freeway to get stoned and listen to rock 'n' roll—is that what it has all been about? And someone, thinking maybe to help feed us, brought a split-open crate of dirty, wilted cabbage heads. They got kicked around in the dust until they rolled under cars and were forgotten.

Some call us Woodstock West, but we are not. Woodstock was a three-day encampment at which cooperation was necessary for survival; it was an event only because it became an event. The Altamont crowd is *demanding* that an event come to pass, be delivered, in a single day; should it go bad—well, it'll be over by evening. And it's four months later, and it's California, where inevitably everything is that wee but significant bit less known, less sure, less safe. . . .

And more political; if concert isn't the right word for the day, festival isn't either. The week's maneuverings, still known only by rumor, have raised a hard edge of suspicion; the day's vibes include aggressive paranoid frequencies that demand self-justification. Some come in bitter mourning for two Chicago Black Panthers shot to death just days before; a concert without confrontation would be frivolous escapism for them. But it is more than the radicals; large segments of the crowd share a dangerous desire to tighten up that festival idea a few notches, to move to a new level—just how weird can you stand it, brother, before your love will crack?

It isn't that the morning is not a groove; it is, friendly enough and loose. But . . . but what? There is too much of something; is it the people, the dope, the tension? Maybe it is the *wanting*, the concentration, not just of flesh, but of unfulfilled desire, of hope for (or is it fear of) deliverance. ("There must be some way out of here, said the joker to the thief; there's too much confusion, I can't get no relief.") What is our oppression that in escaping it we so oppress ourselves? Have we jammed ourselves together on these sere hills miles from home hoping to find a way out of such masses? If that is our paradox, is Altamont our self-made trap? And yet . . . might we just, in acting out the paradox so intensely, transcend it?

The Jefferson Airplane are on stage, knocking out "3/5's of a Mile in 9/10's of a Second" with a mad fury—

> *Do away with people blowing my mind,*
> *Do away with people wasting my precious time;*
> *Take me to a simple place*
> *Where I can easily see my face . . .**

That place is not Altamont—when suddenly all eyes rivet on an upraised pool cue. It is slashing downward, held by a mammoth Hell's Angel, and when it hits its unseen target there is a burst of water as if it had crushed a jellyfish. A wave of horror ripples madly across the crowd. The music stops and the stage is full of Angels in raunchy phalanx. The music starts, falters, stops. Thousands hold their breath and wave pathetic V signs. No one wants the Angels. A few scream, "Pigs, pigs." The odds against the Angels are maybe five-thousand to one, but the crowd is passive and afraid. The Angels stay on stage, sure of their power.

Now something is definitely wrong, but there is no time or space to set it right. The Angels become the villains, but why are they here? They just came, of course, as they always do, but,

---

*"3/5's OF A MILE IN 9/10's OF A SECOND" by Jefferson Airplane. Used by permission of Jefferson Airplane Music.

we hoped, as friends. Since Ken Kesey faced them down and turned them on, San Francisco has had a sentimental romance with the Angels: the consummate outlaws, true rolling stones, street fighting men: they're so bad they're good, went the line. It turns out later that they were actually hired by the Stones on the suggestion of the Dead; their fee, five-hundred-dollars worth of beer. But now their open appetite for violence mocks our unfocused love of peace; their grim solidarity, our fearful hopes of community.

Community? It just doesn't feel like that anymore. Though participants in the whole rite, we are not actively engaged in it; we are spectators who came to "see" the Stones, passive voyeurs hoping, like all voyeurs, that "something" will happen. But since we're just watching, we can say we're not to blame— it's the Stones and the Angels, the Stars, they did it all, so they're to blame, right? The *I Ching* says all communities must have a leader, but every community member must be willing to become that leader at any time.

So we're all voyeurs, but what do you have to do in late 1969 to get 300,000 people to watch it?

> *Now the rovin' gambler he was very bored*
> *Trying to create a next world war*
> *He found a promoter who nearly fell off the floor*
> *He said, "I've never engaged in this kind of*
>   *thing before,*
> *But, yes, I think it can be very easily done,*
> *We'll just put some bleachers out in the sun,*
> *And have it on Highway 61!"**

BOB DYLAN

The day drags on. Many leave; as many more arrive. Invisibly and inevitably the crowd squeezes toward the stage until the first fifty yards around it are suffocatingly dense. Occasionally it becomes too much for someone, and while twitching in the grip of some apocalyptic vision ("We are all going to die, we are all going to die, right here, right here, we've been tricked!"), he is carried by friends to the medical tent for some Thorazine and, if he's lucky, some thoughtful attention.

Darkness begins to fall. "The Stones are here." "I saw

*"HIGHWAY 61 REVISITED (Bob Dylan) © MCMLXV by M. Witmark & Sons. Used by permission of Warner Bros. Music. All rights reserved.

their helicopter." "Somebody said they're not gonna show." The lights come on, and a new wave sweeps thousands more toward the stage. The stage itself is so full that it is sagging in the center. The Angels continue their random attacks. "The Stones are here." "That's why they turned on the lights."

In fact, they are—packed into a tiny trailer filled with stale smoke and spilled food. Charley's happy; he needs only to get through this final set and he can go home to Shirley and Serafina. Mick is upset; as he got off the helicopter a freak had rushed him, screaming, "I hate you, I hate you," then punched him in the face. For all his presence, Mick Jagger is not fearless; on tour, when the engine of one small chartered plane had flamed briefly as it coughed to a start, Mick leapt from his seat, crying that the plane was about to explode. Keith, up all night and in the trailer all day, is exhausted. Crying girls peer and shout through the small screen windows. Jo Bergman is huddled in a corner waiting for it to be over. Ronnie cracks nervous jokes.

It is time. Surrounded by security men, they squeeze the few yards to a tent directly behind the stage. Mick Taylor, Keith, and Bill tune up. A dozen Angels stand guard, punching at faces that peek through holes in the canvas. They are ready. The Angels form a wedge; they file between two equipment trucks, up four steps, and they are there. It is fully dark now but for the stage; in its incandescence, the Rolling Stones are as fine as ever. Mick bows low, sweeping his Uncle Sam hat wide in an ironic circle, and on Keith's signal, the band begins "Jumping Jack Flash." That incredible moment is there again. In those first seconds when Keith's shirt is sparkling, and Charley has just set his big cymbal shimmering with a snap of his right wrist, and Mick bends forward biting out the first defiant words, that enormous pressure of wants, material and spiritual, dissolves—phisst! like that in thin air. For it is just that moment, that achievement of perfect beauty after impossible trial, that is the object of all those longings.

> *'Cause it's all right now,*
> *In fact it's a gas,*
> *I'm Jumping Jack Flash,*
> *It's a gas gas gas!*

And then it is irrevocably gone. Four Angels flash from behind the amps, one vaulting almost over Charley's head. One jumps from the stage, and the crowd scatters into itself in total panic. There appears to be a fight. Then it seems to be over. The music goes on. Again: more Angels, this time wandering around among the Stones. They stop playing.

"Fellows, fellows," says Mick, "move back, won't you, fellows?" His sarcasm gets him through, and they start again. Trouble for the third time, and it is serious. Two Angels (I saw two) wade deep into the crowd. There are screams. Rows of faces fishtail away before these thugs from some very modern nightmare. Boos rise from the mass of the crowd who can't see what's wrong and who just want the show to go on. The band starts again, but something unmistakably weird is still going on down in front. A few kids escape to the stage, streaking to the safety of its far corners. Sam comes out. He has been begging this crowd all day for cooperation; his voice is flat and hoarse.

"This is an important announcement. Someone has been hurt and a doctor is leaving the stage right now; that's him with his arm raised, he's got a green jacket on. Will you please let him through. Someone has been badly hurt."

Security men are begging that all those who do not absolutely need to be on the stage leave it. I leave, not unhappily, and walk through the burnt-out campfires, small piles of trash, and rakishly tilted motorcycles behind the stage, then up a slope where the kids are standing on cars, maybe thirty to a car. A girl comes by asking for her friends; she has cut her leg on barbed wire and wants to go home, but she lost her friends with the car at noon.

The Stones are going again, and the crowd is with them. We can't see them, but the music sounds good—not great, not free festival great, but no one hopes for that anymore. It is enough that it is here. Around me a few people are dancing gently. The morning's dope is wearing off; all the trips are nearly over. We do glimpse the basket flying through the air, trailing petals. We all cheer one last massive cheer. Friends find friends; the crowd becomes fragments that get into cars that back up on the freeway for miles and for hours. Luckily it is only about eight; but it feels like the very end of the night. The only want left is for rest. I realize that the Grateful Dead did not get a chance to play and figure that I won't go to any more of these things.

In the days that follow, the free concert becomes "the disaster at Altamont." There is wide disagreement on what hap-

pened and what it meant; everyone, it seems, had their own day, and that was, we all say, one of the problems. The only common emotion is disappointment and impotent sorrow. "If only . . . if only. . . ." The papers report that there were three births (though later the figure cannot be substantiated) and four deaths. Mark Feiger, twenty-two, and Richard Savlov, twenty-two, friends who had recently moved to Berkeley from New Jersey, were killed when a car on its way out to the freeway plowed into their campfire hours after the concert was over. A young man with long hair, moustache, and sideburns, with a metal cross through his pierced right ear, still listed as "John Doe," stumbled stoned into an irrigation canal and drowned. Another, a young black man, Meredith Hunter, was stabbed, kicked, and beaten by Angels right before the stage while the Stones were playing. His body was battered so badly that doctors knew, the moment they reached him, there was no chance to save him.

So far, no murder charges have been brought. It was not until a week later, when someone asked me about it, that I even considered the possibility that the police, whom no one would have wanted at Altamont in the morning, would actually investigate the horrendous act that closed it and bring any person or persons to trial. We all seemed beyond the law at Altamont, out there willingly, all 300,000 of us, Stones and Angels included, and on our own. And anyway the tour is over.

> Dontcha panic
> Dontcha panic
> Give it one more try
> Dontcha panic
> Dontcha panic
> Give it one more try
> Sit down
> Shut up
> Don't dare cry
> Things'll get better if you really try
> So dontcha panic
> Dontcha panic
> Give it one more try
> Try on!*

—"One More Try"

Michael Lydon, in 1971 and 1990.

AFTERWORD TO THE CITADEL UNDERGROUND EDITION

Soon after I finished *Rock Folk* I began playing music myself, greatly inspired by the musicians whose portraits I had painted. Now I have been a professional for fifteen years. Aside from the many small shifts in perspective that passing years bring to everyone, this change from listener to player has most altered my point of view on *Rock Folk*.

The superb electric sounds of 1960s music utterly overwhelmed me. Men and women, most of them my own age, sang freedom to me and I lapped it up. "He not busy being born is busy dying," "All you need is love," "Shake, everybody, shake"—I couldn't close my ears, or my heart and mind, to such exciting ideas. In the din of the Fillmore I heard a beckoning whisper: "You can do what we're doing!"

Having succumbed to the sirens, now I know how hard they work to make their song enchanting. It takes passion and perseverance to mould a memorable musical style; luck and pluck to survive in the non-stop competition of show business. My years slugging it out in the trenches have tremendously increased my respect for my seven subjects who made it—so young!—over the top to success.

I am delighted that *Rock Folk*, my first book, is being born again at age twenty. May this second life last forever!

M.L.
New York City
April, 1990